# SIR PHILIP SIDNEY
## REPRESENTATIVE ELIZABETHAN

## HIS LIFE AND WRITINGS

SIR PHILIP SIDNEY 1554-1586
(Artist unknown)

# Sir Philip Sidney

## Representative Elizabethan

### His Life and Writings

FREDERICK S. BOAS
O.B.E., Hon. LL.D., Hon. D.Lit., F.R.S.L.

NEW YORK / RUSSELL & RUSSELL

FIRST PUBLISHED IN 1956
REISSUED, 1970, BY RUSSELL & RUSSELL
A DIVISION OF ATHENEUM PUBLISHERS, INC.
BY ARRANGEMENT WITH STAPLES PRESS LIMITED, LONDON
L. C. CATALOG CARD NO: 79-102470
PRINTED IN THE UNITED STATES OF AMERICA

# CONTENTS

# PREFACE

It is merely a chance, though a happy one, that this book appears within the 400th twelvemonth anniversary of the birth of Philip Sidney in 1554. Having spent many years in the study of the Elizabethans, especially the dramatists, I have here sought to interpret one of its most representative figures, whose own career had in it much of dramatic significance. While writing in the light of recent scholarship I have had in view not Elizabethan specialists but those who are anxious to see Sidney's complex character and diversified achievement in a broad perspective.

From Fulke Greville, down the years Sidney has never lacked his devotees. But the past half-century may claim to have been specially fruitful in its tributes. Bertram Dobell's article in *The Quarterly Review* (October 1909) announcing his discovery of manuscripts of the Old *Arcadia* started a new era in the criticism of the romance. It anticipated the publication in 1912 of the 1590 version of the revised *Arcadia* in Professor Albert Feuillerat's first volume of *The Complete Works of Sir Philip Sidney* in the Cambridge Classics series. This fine piece of scholarship was crowned in the fourth volume in 1920 by the printing of the Old *Arcadia* from the Clifford manuscript. It was thus made possible for scholars generally to compare the two versions. The most important outcome of the debate that has ensued has been Professor R. W. Zandvoort's study published at Amsterdam in 1929. He sides with Feuillerat in giving the preference to the revised *Arcadia*. My own preference, with qualifications, is with Dobell, for the compact structure of the original romance. For my quotations from it in Feuillerat's reproduction I wish to express my indebtedness to the Syndics of the Cambridge University Press, and my hope that it will become increasingly familiar. For readers not versed in the vagaries of Elizabethan spelling I have given quotations from this and other works of Sidney in modern form.

Another work published by the Cambridge University Press is *The Life of Sir Philip Sidney* by Professor A. W.

7

Wallace of Toronto (1915). Wallace threw fresh light on Sidney's boyhood by his discovery of Marshall's Book of Accounts at Penshurst. On his adult activities he gave an illuminating account of the contemporary political background. The late Miss Mona Wilson's *Sir Philip Sidney* (1931) is a well-balanced study, with a useful bibliographical basis. C. Henry Warren in *Sir Philip Sidney* (1936) has laid stress on the conflict in him between the poet and the man of action. To these and others mentioned in my text or footnotes every writer on Sidney must be under an obligation.[1]

My own study aims at giving an all-round presentation of Sir Philip. Thus in his literary aspect besides his major works I have discussed some of his metrical experiments in the eclogues and the translations and have dealt more fully than usual with *The Lady of May*. In *The Defence of Poesie* I have tried to separate what is permanently valuable in Sidney's criticism from his transient verdicts on contemporary poets and playwrights. In this connexion I have specially noted incidental theatrical references in the *Arcadia*. While supporting to the full the high poetic claim of *Astrophel and Stella* and its autobiographical basis, I have pointed out what seems to me the difficulty of reconciling it with other aspects of Sidney's life. It is the major paradox of which there seem to me various minor instances in his career. But this makes him all the more a, perhaps the, representative Elizabethan. That age, with all its glories and graces, had its failings, and inconsistencies. Thus Philip Sidney is its more characteristic product if weaknesses are not overlooked which were but a foil to his versatile genius and his magnetic personality.

F.S.B.

---

[1] My text was completed before the publication of Mr John Buxton's *Sir Philip Sidney and the English Renaissance*.

# CHAPTER I

# BIRTH AND PARENTAGE

'I am a Dudley in blood, that Duke's daughter's son, and do acknowledge, though in all truth I may justly affirm that I am by my father's side of ancient and always well-esteemed and well-matched gentry, yet I do acknowledge, I say, that my chiefest honour is to be a Dudley, and truly am glad to have cause to set forth the nobility of that blood whereof I am descended.'

The 'cause' which led Philip Sidney thus proudly to vindicate his parentage, especially on the maternal side, was the attack in 1584 in the scurrilous pamphlet, *Leicester's Commonwealth*, on the Dudley family and in particular on its head, the Earl of Leicester, as the real ruler of England. Leicester's father, the Earl of Warwick, had been created Duke of Northumberland in October 1551. He had taken the lead in the plot by which his daughter-in-law, Lady Jane Grey, was to succeed to the throne, on Edward VI's death, instead of his sister Mary, and had paid the penalty with his own life and those of Lady Jane and her husband, Lord Guildford Dudley.

It was fortunate for Northumberland's daughter, Lady Mary Dudley, that she had been married in March 1551 to Sir Henry Sidney, who had retained the royal favour under successive sovereigns. Born on July 20th, 1529, at nine years of age, he was appointed a henchman by Henry VIII, and became an intimate companion of his son, Edward. When in 1547 'that sweet prince', as Henry Sidney calls him, succeeded to the throne, the young King showered favours on him. He was appointed one of the four principal Gentlemen of the Bedchamber, Cup-Bearer and Chief-Cypherer, and was granted estates and stewardships. These were confirmed by Mary when she became Queen. He had been knighted in October 1551.

That Sir Henry merited this exceptional recognition is attested by distinguished contemporaries, even if allowance has to be made for the flowery extravagance of Tudor complimentary style. Holinshed declares that 'this noble gentleman for his forwardness in all good actions was, as it were, the paragon of the Court by reason of the many good gifts which God had bestowed on him every way'. There follows a catalogue of these 'good gifts', physical and otherwise. Similarly Fulke Greville records that Sir Henry Sidney 'was a man of excellent natural wit, large heart, sweet conversation, and such a Governor as sought not to make an end of the State in himself, but to plant his own ends in the prosperity of his country'. Of his wife, Lady Mary, the biographer adds, 'As she was a woman by descent of great Nobility, so was she by nature of a large ingenuous spirit'. The 'well-mixed offspring' of this pair was born at Pensnurst on November 30th, 1554, a quarter before five in the morning. He had a remarkable set of godparents for his christening. King Philip of Spain had a few months before been escorted to England for his marriage with Queen Mary by an embassy which included the Earl of Bedford and Sir Henry Sidney. This intimacy was prolonged by the presence at the font of the Earl and 'the great King, from whom the infant derived his name, Philip'. The Duchess of Northumberland, his godmother, was the widow of the Duke who had sought to keep Queen Mary from the throne.

Of Philip's early childhood there is very scant record, but events of importance were happening in his family. In May 1556 Sir Henry accompanied to Ireland the new Lord Deputy, Lord Fitzwalter, afterwards Earl of Sussex. He saw service in Ulster, and acted as Lord Justice when the Lord Deputy was absent from Ireland. Lady Mary joined him in Dublin, but on the accession of Elizabeth to the throne in 1558 she was summoned to Court, where her loyalty to the Queen was tempered by outspoken independence. Their association had a disastrous consequence. In 1562 Elizabeth had a severe attack of smallpox, during which she was devotedly nursed by Lady Mary, who caught the infection. Though she recovered, the disease left her permanently disfigured, and the former beauty of the Court retired for the most part into solitary life at Penshurst, where on November 19th 1563, her second son, Robert, was born.

Meanwhile Sir Henry had been recalled from Ireland. Elizabeth did not show to the Sidney family the same favour as her predecessors. But she was sufficiently acute to recognize their abilities and make use of them when it suited her policies. In the summer of 1560 she appointed Sir Henry Lord President of the Marches of Wales. It proved to be a very congenial office. As Sir Henry afterwards stated, 'A happy place of government it is, for a better people to govern, or better subjects to their Sovereign Europe holdeth not.' He continues, in what now sounds pictistic phraseology, it is 'most happy for the commodity that I have by the authority of that place to do good every day, if I have grace, to one or other'. There is sufficient testimony that Sir Henry discharged his duties as President in the spirit of these words. His places of residence were Ludlow Castle, and Tickenhall House, Bewdley, where on October 27th, 1561, was born his daughter Mary, whose name was to become so inseparably linked with that of Philip. But Sir Henry's activities were not confined to his Presidential area. He was sent in 1562 on various missions, to Catherine de Medici, to Mary, Queen of Scots, and, with his brother-in-law, the Earl of Warwick, to the assistance of Louis de Condé, the Huguenot leader, though he went only as far as Havre. They were, in fact, all short-time absences but they testified to the trust placed in him by William Cecil's not over-friendly Government.

Meanwhile little Philip was growing up under his mother's care among the rural surroundings of their home in Kent, celebrated later in a poem on Penshurst by Ben Jonson, addressed to Robert Sidney, of which a few lines run:

The painted partridge lies in every field,
And for thy mess is willing to be kill'd.
And if the high-swol'n Medway fail thy dish,
Thou has thy ponds, that pay thee tribute fish.

\*        \*        \*

Thou hast thy orchard fruit, thy garden flowers
Fresh as the air, and new as are thy hours.
The early cherry, with the later plum,

Fig, grape and quince, each in his time doth come:
The blushing apricot and woolly peach,
Hang on thy walls that every child may reach.

If only we could have had a companion piece addressed by
Shakespeare to Philip! Some impressions of this early en-
vironment must have stamped themselves upon the mind of
a sensitive child, and in the description in Book I, Chapter 2
(1590), of Kalander's house there appears to be a reminiscence of Penshurst itself:

> (It) was built of fair and strong stone, not affecting so
> much any extraordinary kind of fineness as an honourable
> representing of a firm stateliness. The lights, doors, and
> stairs rather directed to the use of the guest than to the
> eye of the artificer: and yet as the one chiefly heeded so
> the other not neglected . . . all more lasting than beauti-
> ful, but that the consideration of the exceeding lastingness
> made the eyes believe it was exceeding beautiful.

# CHAPTER II

# SHREWSBURY SCHOOL – VISIT TO OXFORD

Owing to his father's appointment as Lord President Philip's schooling was to be at a far cry from his home in Kent. Sir Henry's jurisdiction included Shrewsbury to which he had to pay frequent official visits. Hence it arose that he sent Philip to the 'free grammar school' of that town, which under the headmastership of Thomas Ashton, a Fellow of Trinity College, Cambridge, gained a high reputation. Appointed in June 1561 Ashton remained in office till his resignation in 1571. Philip entered the school on October 17th, 1564, when he was ten years old. According to the arrangements for boys enrolled from a distance, he was 'tabled' or boarded with a householder, George Leigh. From February 2nd till November 1st he had to be at school from six o'clock in the morning till four-thirty in the afternoon; during the three other months from seven o'clock till five-thirty. The curriculum was almost entirely in Latin, and it is of interest to note that the school has retained its pre-eminence as a centre of classical education into recent days. B. J. Kennedy was a worthy nineteenth-century successor to Ashton.

On the same day as Philip there was enrolled at the school Fulke Greville, the son of a wealthy Warwickshire landowner, who was to become his life-long friend and his biographer. In his description of Philip as a boy some discount must again be made for the rotund style of the period, which otherwise might leave an impression, far from intended, of youthful priggishness:

> Of whose youth I will report no other words but this: that though I lived with him and knew him from a child, yet I never knew him other than a man: with such staidness of mind, lovely and familiar gravity, as carried grace and reverence above greater years. His talk ever of knowledge, and his very play tending to enrich his mind. So as even his teachers found something in him to observe, and learn, above that which they had usually read or

13

taught. Which eminence, by nature and industry made his worthy father style Sir Philip in my hearing (though unseen) *Lumen familiae suae.*

As will be seen, versatile as was Philip with his pen, there are gaps in his records of his experiences, and in his own writings he throws little light upon his schooldays. It is therefore all the more fortunate that there has been preserved at Penshurst the manuscript Book of Accounts kept by Thomas Marshall, appointed by Sir Henry to attend upon Philip, from December 4th, 1565, to September 29th, 1566. This was discovered by Professor M. W. Wallace of University College, Toronto, and was printed in full as an appendix to his *The Life of Sir Philip Sidney.* It covers approximately the second of Philip's school years. Much of it is occupied with expenses on Philip's attire and accoutrements, including ii*$^d$* 'for mendinge of his dagger' and xii*$^d$* 'for trimming of his rapier and false scaberd'. Even as a schoolboy Philip must have presented a courtly appearance. Other entries arise out of his studies. One is viii*$^d$* 'for two quier of paper, for example bookes, frases [i.e. phrases] and sentences in latyne and frenche'. This is of special interest as it shows that a modern language was included in the timetable. The combination of humanist and Puritan elements in the Shrewsbury educational system is forcibly illustrated in the entry of xx*$^d$* for 'a Virgile' immediately followed by one of iiii*$^d$* for 'Calvines chatachisme'.

There is one important feature, however, of the Shrewsbury educational régime which has no place in Marshall's record, possibly because Philip was as yet too junior to be concerned with it. It was a notable part of the Renaissance Classical training to include in it the acting by boys and undergraduates of plays, chiefly in Latin. Shrewsbury school was advantageously provided for this – somewhat like Bradfield in our own day for its Greek performances – by having a quarry in the neighbourhood, where a play was staged at Whitsuntide. Whether or not Philip in his later school years took part in this as an actor, it must have started his interest in dramatic productions about which he was to discourse in his *Defence of Poesie.*

Though these performances had a didactic origin they gradually everywhere acquired also an entertainment value, all the more because the holiday periods were limited. But Philip, probably owing to his lofty family connexions, seems to have had no difficulty in procuring additional *exeats*. While his father and mother were waiting at Chester after November 17th, 1565, in the hope of being able to cross to Ireland, where Sir Henry had been appointed Lord Deputy, Philip with two school friends was allowed to pay them a visit which ended on December 3rd. Six months later there was a more unpleasant cause of an exodus for three weeks to the houses of Sir Andrew Corbet and Sir Richard Newton. The plague had attacked Shrewsbury. Marshall describes this on May 30th, 1566, as 'When the scholars were sick', and on June 21st he has an entry of 12$^d$ 'for perfumes to ayre the chambre with when we came furthe of the countrie after the younge gentlemen were recovered'.

The later summer of this year was to make ample amends to Philip for what must have been the discomfort of an enforced and hurried leave-taking. Towards the end of July he received a summons from his uncle, the Earl of Leicester, to come to his great house, Kenilworth Castle. From there he was to be one of the company attending Leicester, who was to welcome Queen Elizabeth on a visit to the University of Oxford, of which the Earl was the Chancellor. A first attempt to reach Kenilworth by Philip and his party was for some unknown reason a failure. After starting on July 24th they were turned back and had to spend the night of the 27th again at Shrewsbury. Worst of all the long spell of riding had brought forth on Philip what Marshall calls 'merrygalls', a sore which needed treatment by a box of ointment and a period of rest. On August 14th Philip again rode forth, with Marshall and another younger attendant, Randal Colcott, and accompanied by his headmaster, Ashton, with two dependants. At this second time of asking they reached Kenilworth on the 17th, and Marshall at once rode over to Coventry, where Leicester was staying, to speak with him 'for the Knowledge of Mr Philip's apparel'. The Earl was evidently anxious that his young kinsman's appearance should do them both credit, and he munificently ordered for him from his London tailor a very decorative set of garments of which Marshall gives a list.[1] But it was not only to Philip's outward show that Leicester paid attention. When after five days' residence at the Castle his nephew on August 22nd set out for the University city it was under the care of Thomas Wilson, whose treatise, *The Arte of Rhetorique*, dealt with linguistic problems which would interest so intelligent a young student as Philip. And at Oxford itself for almost the whole of his stay, from August 25th to September 8th, he was lodged with John Bridgewater, Rector of Lincoln College and domestic chaplain to Lord Leicester. Under the classical version of his name, Aquepontus, he gained a wide reputation for theological works in Latin whose trend was opposed to the Puritan doctrines favoured at Shrewsbury. Anything in the form of religious controversy would probably be avoided on this festal occasion, which began with the entrance of the Queen, accompanied by a glittering crowd of notables, on August 31st. Welcomed in speeches by academic and civic dignitaries she was escorted in processional triumph to Christ Church. A youth of Philip's sensitive perceptions could scarcely fail to be impressed by so imposing a spectacle, and he may have taken the opportunity of improving his Latin by listening to some of the academic discussions arranged in the Queen's honour. But with the emphasis placed at his school on the acting of plays one would be inclined to assume that his primary interest would be in the evening performances at Christ Church. The first and last of these, *Marcus Geminus*, a Latin comedy, and *Progne*, a Latin tragedy, were of 'the House' vintage. Of greater interest was the two-part play, *Palamon and Areïte*, by Richard Edwardes, Master of the Children of the Chapel Royal. It has not survived, but from the accounts of it, and from the connexion of its subject with Chaucer's *The Knight's Tale*, one could have wished that Philip had recorded some esti mate of it as he was to do in *The Defence of Poesie* of *Gorboduc*, acted four years earlier at the Inner Temple. But of this eventful visit to Oxford, under august auspices, there is no reminiscence in his own writings. Paradoxically, however, if Professor Wallace's plausible conjecture is right, he has immortalized a simple, unrehearsed incident on his return journey. Marshall records that on Sunday, September 8th, he gave 12ᵈ 'by Mr Philip's commandement to a blind harper, who was in the service of Sir William Holles'. There are not many blind harpers, and it may well be that Philip had this one in mind when he wrote the touching words in the *Defence*, 'I never heard the old song of Percy and Douglas that I found not my heart moved more than with a trumpet, and yet is it sung but by some blind crowder with no rougher voice than crude style.'

It must have been difficult for Philip after such exciting experiences to settle down again to normal school routine. But he would have been helped in this by the letter which he received from his father in the course of this year, 1566, from which the following are extracts:

Son Philip, I have received two letters from you, one written in Latin, the other in French: which I take in good part, and will you to exercise that practice of learning often; for that will stand you in most stead in that profession of life that you are born to live in. And now, since this is my first letter that ever I did write to you, I will not that it be all empty of some advice which my natural care of you provoketh me to wish you to follow, as documents to you in this your tender age.

Let your first action be the lifting up of your mind to Almighty God by hearty prayer; and feelingly digest the words you speak in prayer, with continual meditation and thinking of Him to whom you pray, and of the matter for which you pray. And use this as an ordinary act, and at an ordinary hour; whereby the time itself shall put you in remembrance to do that you are accustomed to do in that time.

Apply your study to such hours as your discreet master doth assign you earnestly . . . And mark the sense and the matter of that you do read as well as the words; so shall you both enrich your tongue with words and your wit with matter, and judgment will grow as years grow in you. Be humble and obedient to your masters, for, unless you frame yourself to obey others – yea, and feel in yourself what obedience is, you shall never be able to teach others to obey you. Be courteous of gesture and affable to all men, with diversity of reverence according to the dignity of the person; there is nothing that winneth so much with so little cost.

Use moderate diet so as, after your meal, you may find your wit fresher, and not duller, and your body lively and not more heavy. Seldom drink wine, and yet sometimes do, lest, being enforced to drink upon the sudden you should find yourself inflamed. Use exercise of body; yet such as is without peril to your bones or joints.

*     *     *

Above all things tell no untruth; no, not in trifles. The custom of it is naughty . . . For there cannot be a greater reproach to a gentleman than to be accounted a liar. Study and endeavour yourself to be virtuously occupied. So shall you make such a habit of well-doing in you as you shall not know how to do evil, though you would.

After such a comprehensive exhortation to a boy aged twelve, Sir Henry need scarcely have ended with so conditional a signature as 'Your loving father, so long as you live in the fear of God.' In a less restrained postscript Lady Mary added that she would not divert her son's attention from his noble father's letters by one from her. She will only 'first bless you, with my desire to God to plant you in His grace and secondarily, warn you to have always before the eyes of your mind these excellent counsels of my lord, your dear father, and that you fail not continually, once in four of five days, to read them over'. She ends with whole-hearted affection, 'Farewell, my little Philip, and once again the Lord bless you! Your loving mother, Mary Sidney.'

Whether or not Philip obeyed his mother's instructions to read over his father's precepts at regular short intervals, they set a standard by which, allowing for human frailty, his whole career was to be shaped.

# CHAPTER III

# UNDERGRADUATE AT CHRIST CHURCH, OXFORD

At what exact date Philip came again to Oxford, not as a visitor, but as an undergraduate at Christ Church, is not known, but it was probably in 1568, though possibly in the previous year. If one may judge by his later writings, all the subjects of the more advanced academic course, the *Trivium*, grammar, rhetoric and logic would have an attraction for him. But, on his own testimony, like a medieval predecessor, Chaucer's Clerk of Oxenford, he was specially drawn to Aristotle. As he was to write in 1574 to Hubert Languet, 'Of Greek literature I wish to learn only so much as shall suffice for the perfect understanding of Aristotle. For though translations are made almost daily, still I suspect they do not declare the meaning of the author plainly or aptly enough.' That Philip owed a real debt to Aristotle will appear later, but it will also be shown that his suspicion of translations was justified, and that by them and by commentaries he was considerably misled.[1] That Philip took part in the 'disputations' which were then one of the preliminaries to a degree is evidenced by a statement of his contemporary, Richard Carew. 'Being a scholar in Oxford of fourteen years age and three years standing, upon a wrong conceived opinion touching my sufficiency, I was there called to dispute extempore (*impar congressus Achilli*) with the matchless Sir Philip Sidney, in presence of the Earls Leicester, Warwick, and divers other personages.'

As at Shrewsbury Philip had been fortunate in such a headmaster as Ashton, so at Christ Church he was under the care of a succession of very scholarly tutors. The first was Thomas Thornton, who became a Canon of the Cathedral, and later Vice-Chancellor of the University. The second was Thomas Cooper, the eminent lexicographer, who had been Dean of Christ Church since 1567, when he also became

---

[1] On his own lost translations of two Books of Aristotle's *Rhetoric*, see p. 160.

19

Vice-Chancellor, and ultimately Bishop of Winchester. He was succeeded as Philip's tutor by Nathaniel Baxter, who later held clerical posts at Youghal in Ireland and Troy in Monmouthshire, and who as late as 1606 was to publish a poem dedicated to his pupil's memory, *Sir Philip Sidney's Ovrania*.

It was on behalf of Thornton that Philip wrote his first extant letter in English, to Sir William Cecil (afterwards Lord Burghley). Thornton had been promised the first vacant canonry, but a rival candidate appeared in the person of another gifted Christ Church scholar, Tobie Matthew. With what was later to prove characteristic whole-hearted impulsiveness Philip addressed the Secretary of State:

> Right Honourable: I am forced for better expedition to use an unaccustomed manner of writing to you, the cause proceding from a report of some whom neither can I judge friendly to myself, nor yet indifferent towards him from whom they seek by malice to prevent and detain his worthy preferment, sued for and obtained by his honourable benefactors, I mean my singular good Lord, my Lord of Leicester, and especially yourself, by whose favour (atained by the request of my friends and his desert towards me, assisted by the worthiness of his life and learning) Mr Thornton, my reader, hath unto him granted the next preferment of a canonry in this College of Christ Church. . . . These are therefore most humbly to request such your wonted favour as neither your honourable benefit may be revoked, my humble and learnest suit prevented, neither the person himself so discredited but that he may with your favour enjoy his advowson, by your means obtained and yourself promised.

This letter, dated from Oxford, February 20th, 1569/70, was successful in its appeal, but Matthew also in his turn became a Canon of Christ Church and ultimately Archbishop of York.

There was to be a less prosperous issue to a Sidney correspondence with Cecil on a matter touching Philip more intimately than the preferment of his tutor, a marriage alliance between him and the Secretary's daughter, Anne.

At first all promised well. On August 2nd, 1568, Sir Henry, before returning to Ireland, paid a visit to Oxford where he received the degree of M.A. Writing to him on August 10th, Cecil, after thanking him for his commendations to 'my wife and your little maid, my daughter' wishes 'health to my good lady, your wife, and increase of all goodness to your son, my darling master Philip'. As Philip's studies had been interrupted at Shrewsbury by his various excursions, so his father now took him away with him from Oxford for a month to Wales. Whereupon Cecil on September 3rd wrote to reproach Sir Henry with having 'carried away your son and my scholar from Oxford not only from his book but from the commodity . . . to have pleasured both me and my wife'. On November 30th Sir Henry sent to Cecil from Ireland his 'most hearty commendations to yourself, my lady, and my sweet jewel, your daughter'. On January 29th, 1569, Cecil replied, 'Your Philip is here, in whom I take more comfort than I do openly utter for avoiding of wrong interpretation. He is worthy to be loved, and so I do love him as he were my son.' Such an expression might well justify Sir Henry in making a proposal of a marriage contract between Philip and Anne, but Cecil's interest thereupon cooled, and the protracted negotiations ended with the betrothal of Anne in August 1571 to the undisciplined but very wealthy young Earl of Oxford. There is no allusion to matters of such family moment in the two grateful and respectfully affectionate Latin letters of Philip to Cecil, dated March 12th and July 8th, 1569, the first products that have survived of his pen, preceding his English letter of February in the next year.

At what date Philip left Oxford without taking a degree is not known. And it is in no spirit of jealousy for my own University that I query Professor Wallace's acceptance of 'contemporary evidence' for his migration for a time to Cambridge. It is true that George Whetstone in his verse elegy upon Philip, some time after his death, said in one of his prose glosses, 'He was in his time and for his continuance reputed the best scholar in Cambridge.' But Whetstone, who attributed Spenser's *Shepheardes Kalender* to Sidney,[1] and

[1] See T. C. Izard, *George Whetstone* (1942), p. 255.

who was not himself at either University, may in his questionable complimentary statement have confused the two. Lawrence Humphreys, Vice-Chancellor of Oxford, in a memorial Latin poem represents Philip's shade as addressing Cambridge, '*Hospes eram, gratum praebuit hospitium,*' whereas he continues, '*Oxoniae matri quid dicam?*' Is there not intended here a contrast between his *alma mater* Oxford, and Cambridge which on some special occasion made him an honoured guest?

# CHAPTER IV

# CONTINENTAL TRAVEL – FRIENDSHIP WITH HUBERT LANGUET

It was not, in any case, at an English University that Sidney's education, as it will henceforward be appropriate to call him, was to be completed. On May 25th, 1572, the Queen granted him a licence to go out of England into parts beyond the seas for two years 'for his attaining the knowledge of foreign languages'. He was to proceed first to Paris, to be under the eye of the ambassador Sir Francis Walsingham, to whose care the Earl of Leicester commended him in a letter more benevolent than complimentary: 'He is young and raw, and no doubt shall find those countries and the demeanours of the people somewhat strange unto him; and therefore your good advice and counsel shall greatly behove him for his better direction.' Leicester might have been surprised to learn that, as Lodowick Bryskett, one of his companions, afterwards reported, the 'graver sort of courtiers' were 'no less delighted with his ready and witty answers than astonished to hear him speak the French language so well and aptly having been so short a while in the country'. The French King himself, Charles IX, was so charmed by him that he created him a Gentleman Ordinary of the Bedchamber and Baron de Sidenay.

With the marriage on August 18th of the King's sister Margaret de Valois and Henry of Navarre it seemed as if a close were being brought to the strife between Roman Catholics and Huguenots. But the assassination of Coligny, the Huguenot leader, followed by the massacre of Saint Bartholomew destroyed all such hopes. Sidney himself in the safe haven of the British embassy was in no personal danger, but the scenes of horror enacted so near him left a permanent impression and strengthened his Protestant sympathies.

When the news of the massacre reached London the Privy Council wrote to Walsingham directing him 'to procure for the Lord Wharton and Mr Philip Sidney the King's license and safe-conduct' to leave France and return home. But the Ambassador had already sent Sidney away with a party travelling to Germany. His first place of residence there was at Frankfurt in the house of the printer Andrew Wechel, where Hubert Languet was also an inmate. Sidney had in all probability already become acquainted with this scholar-diplomat in Paris, where he was the representative at the Court of Versailles of the Elector of Saxony. Now aged fifty-four he was one of the most eminent Huguenot leaders, and had been fortunate in escaping from the St Bartholomew massacre. He was strongly attracted by Sidney's intellectual and moral qualities, and with the distance of the young Englishman from his family influences, Languet assumed the position of his mentor. Hence, when Languet in the spring of 1573 moved as the Elector's representative to the Emperor's Court in Vienna, Sidney prepared to follow him. On his way he stopped at Heidelberg where he began a friendship with another printer, Henry Stephens, who was afterwards to dedicate to him his edition of the New Testament in Greek. At Strassburg he met the scholar John Sturm who showed him courtesies for which he received the thanks of Burghley.

After some months at Vienna Sidney set out on what purported to be a three days' trip to Hungary, which was however extended to several weeks. This led to the beginning of Languet's correspondence in Latin with Sidney,[1] wherein affectionate declarations were mingled with reproaches for his prolonged absence and for the infrequency of his letters. It was no light task for Sidney to satisfy Languet on various counts. He was anxious to keep his young friend's close personal intimacy, to improve his classical scholarship, and to make use of him and his family connexions in the service of the Protestant cause. When therefore Sidney announced his intention of visiting Italy, Languet tried to dissuade him and only gave way when Sidney undertook that he would not go to Rome. Languet gave him introductions to friends at Venice, where the Count of Hanau in particular began a

---

[1] Languet's *Epistolae ad Philippum Sydmaturm* was published at Leyden in 1646 and edited by Lord Hailes in Edinburgh in 1776. A translation into English of most of them, and of Sidney's replies, was furnished by S. A. Pears in London in 1845, with an introductory essay.

helpful intimacy with him. But, as Sidney confessed in a
letter to Languet, he was disappointed with Venice, and thus
was one of the few Englishmen from his day to ours who
have not felt the fascination of the city of lagoons. His
mentor advised him to move to the more sedate atmosphere
of Padua, which with its University was in European eyes
a 'nursery of arts'. And when Sidney, as may be believed,
obeyed Languet's injunction to study especially 'that branch
of moral philosophy which treats of justice and injustice', he
was anticipating Lucentio in *The Taming of the Shrew* who
came to Padua with the purpose of applying himself to that
part of philosophy,

> . . . that treats of happiness
> By virtue specially to be achieved.

And in Sidney's case there does not seem to have been a
Bianca whose charms were to divert him to love in idleness.
But his stay at the time in Padua was only from the middle
of January 1574 to the end of February, when he returned
to Venice. Here Paul Veronese painted his portrait which
he sent to Languet, who at first thought it to be too youthful,
and even later, though he was more appreciative, wished
that the expression had been more cheerful. Its loss is to be
deplored.

The following months were spent mainly between Venice
and Padua, except for short visits to Florence and Genoa.
Probably in August he returned to Vienna, where he fell
seriously ill. On his recovery he spent some time in Poland,
to the regret of the Count of Hanau, who had to leave Vienna
before Sidney came back. On November 27th he wrote to
his uncle, Leicester, giving him a short survey of the political
situation on the Continent.

During the winter of 1574–5 Sidney made another close
friend in the English Resident in Vienna, Edward Wotton,
of whom he was to make a pleasant reminiscence in the
beginning of his *Defence of Poesie*. When Languet had to
accompany the Emperor towards the end of February to
Prague, Sidney followed him there for a few days. But he
was already occupied with plans for his return journey to
England, for which Languet furnished him not only with

letters of introduction but with a financial loan. Heidelberg and Strassburg were revisited, as was also Frankfurt where in May Languet had his last personal intercourse with Sidney on the Continent.

It is somewhat difficult for us today to appreciate fully the emotional quality in the friendship between the two. It was a feature of the Renaissance period which invested masculine relationship with an idealism usually reserved for that between the two sexes. It is this impassioned feeling that binds Shakespeare to his friend, however identified, in the Sonnets, that causes Hamlet to wear Horatio in his 'heart of heart', and that in Beaumont and Fletcher's *The Maid's Tragedy* ties Melantinus to Amintor, with the cry:

The name of friend is more than family,
Or all the world beside.

But, as has already been partly seen, prudent considerations combined with emotional in Languet's attitude towards his ward, and he warned Sidney to cultivate the friendship of Burghley and Walsingham on his arrival in England. Leaving Antwerp on May 31st, accompanied by Edward Wotton who had joined him at Basle, he had a prosperous voyage, and on June 12th could report to the Count of Hanau that he had found all his family well, though they had lost his youngest sister, Ambrosia, in the previous February. This had produced from the Queen an unusually sympathetic letter to Sir Henry, in which after offering him religious consolation, she continued, 'He hath yet left unto you the comfort of one daughter of very good life, whom, if you shall think good to remove from those parts of unpleasant air (if it be so) into better in these parts, and will send her unto us before Easter, or when you shall think good, assure yourself that we will have a special care of her.' This 'daughter of very good life' was Mary, then under fourteen years of age, who was thus summoned into the Court circle, and who later as Countess of Pembroke was to have her name inseparably associated with that of her brother Philip. But if Sir Henry, in sending Mary to London, was obeying what was virtually a royal command, it was not because he thought of his residence in Wales as in an 'unpleasant air'. He was thoroughly happy in his position as Lord President. Lady Mary, on the other hand, suffering from ill-health and financial troubles, was in an aggrieved mood which seems to have persisted even after her son's return.

# CHAPTER V

# WITH HIS FATHER IN IRELAND

It was nine years since Sidney as a boy had visited his uncle Robert's castle at Kenilworth, but then it was merely a temporary halting-place on his way to attend the festivities at Oxford during the Queen's visit in the summer of 1566. By a coincidence, a few months after his return to England, he was again to be his uncle's guest at Kenilworth, but in very different circumstances. From July 9th to 27th, 1575, Elizabeth honoured Leicester by taking up her abode under his roof. She was entertained on an unprecedented scale of lavish splendour with mythological shows, masques, music, sports of all kinds and fireworks in the evenings. Sidney, with his father and mother, was in the Queen's retinue, and must have been an interested spectator but, as with the plays he had seen at Oxford, there is no allusion to the Kenilworth festivities in his writings.

The Queen's 'progress' then continued to Lichfield where on July 31st Sir Henry Sidney was sworn of the Privy Council, and on August 2nd was appointed once again, in spite of his reluctance, Lord Deputy of Ireland, where the situation had been going from bad to worse. Again Sidney, as in his schoolboy days, seems to have seen his father off on his voyage across the Irish Sea. It was probably a stage on their journey north when they arrived at Shrewsbury where the corporation accounts have an item of 7ˢ 2ᵈ for expenses 'to Mr Philip Sidney at his coming to this town with my Lord President, his father'. It must have been a thrill for Philip to be a guest of honour in the city to which about seven years ago he had said goodbye as a schoolboy.

The separation between father and son was not to be for long. The winter of 1575–6 was spent by Sidney in London, where he received a mark of the Queen's favour by being appointed a Cup-Bearer. But his father may well have thought it advantageous to have his support in dealing with the troubles in Connaught, and as a *liaison* with the home

28

Government. By the middle of August Sir Henry speaks of Philip being with him, and he must have been witness of the sternly repressive measures with which the Lord Deputy put down the southern insurgents. Meanwhile, however, his co-operator in the north, the first Earl of Essex, as Earl Marshal, was continuing his losing struggle against the rebels in Ulster. Suddenly Essex in August was stricken with an illness which after a month proved fatal. He had always been deeply attached to Philip, and had sent messages urging him to hasten to his bedside, but from the west of Ireland Philip could not arrive till after the Earl's death in Dublin on September 22nd. He found, however, the following testimony:

> Tell him I send him nothing, but I wish him well, and so well that if God do move both their hearts I wish that he might match with my daughter. I call him son; he is so wise, so virtuous and godly; and if he go on in the course he hath begun, he will be as famous and worthy a gentleman as ever England had.

It would have been happy for Sidney had the first part of the Earl's wish for his future been realised as well as the second. But this would have been at the cost of a series of Elizabethan sonnets that ranks second only to Shakespeare's.

On his return to London Sidney's pen was occupied with a *Discourse on Ireland* (of which only a fragment survives) in which he defended his father's policy, especially in the levy of 'cess' upon all landowners, among whom Sir Henry would have included the Queen's favourite, the Earl of Ormond, till she ordered him to be exempted. Sidney also approved of Sir Henry's measures of severe repression.

> For little [he wrote] is lenity to prevail in minds so possessed, with a natural inconstancy ever to go to a new fortune, with a revengeful hate to all English as to their only conquerors, and that which is most of all with so ignorant obstinacy in papistry, that they do in their souls detest the present government.

None the less he showed his sympathy with the luckless under-dogs. 'Privileged persons be all the rich men of the pale; but burden only lying on the poor, who may groan, for their cry cannot be heard.'

Sir Henry's agent, Edward Waterhouse, on reading the *Discourse*, exclaimed admiringly, 'Let no man compare with Mr Philip's pen.' The Queen's reception of it was doubtless less enthusiastic, but she was now to employ him in a role in which his experience of foreign countries and personalities was to be specially valuable.

# CHAPTER VI

# ELIZABETH'S DIPLOMATIC ENVOY –
## INTEREST IN EXPLORATION –
## LETTER AGAINST THE FRENCH MARRIAGE

On his earlier residence on the Continent Sidney had been a predecessor of those eighteenth-century English notables who completed their education by making the grand tour. Now in February 1577 he was to set forth on a formal continental mission as the Queen's accredited envoy, accompanied by Fulke Greville, Sir Henry Lee and Edward Dyer. He was to convey to the Emperor Rudolph and his mother Elizabeth's condolences on the death of the late Emperor, and similarly to the Counts Palatine, Lewis and Casimir, on the death of their father. On arriving in Brussels, Sidney at once proceeded to Louvain to pay his respects to Don John of Austria, half-brother of King Philip of Spain, and Governor of the Netherlands. From Fulke Greville's account it is evident that even the steely Spanish magnate was overcome by Sidney's personal charm.

> Though at the first, in his Spanish haughteur, he gave him access as by descent to a youth, of grace as to a stranger, and in particular competition (as he conceived) to an enemy; yet after a while that he had taken his just attitude, he found himself so stricken with this extraordinary Planet, that the beholders wondered to see what ingenuous tribute that brave and high-minded Prince paid to his worth; giving more honour and respect to this hopeful young gentleman than to the ambassadors of mighty Princes.

At Heidelberg, the next stage of his journey, Sidney, in the absence of the Elector Lewis, presented the Queen's condolences to his brother Casimir. From there he went to Prague where on Easter Monday he reported to the Emperor the grief of Elizabeth at the loss of so worthy a friend

31

as his father, to which Rudolph replied 'in Latin with very few words'. Next day he had a more delicate task of condoling with the bereaved Empress–Dowager of the Emperor deceased. 'I used but few words, because in truth I saw it bred some trouble unto her to hear him mentioned in that kind.' With even greater cause for agitation was her daughter, who had lost both her father and her husband, King Charles IX of France. Sidney delivered to her a letter from Elizabeth, 'using such speeches as I thought were fit for her double sorrow, and her Majesty's good will unto her . . . Her answer was full of humbleness, but she spake so low that I could not understand many of her words.'

At Prague he also renewed an intimacy with an Oxford contemporary, Edmund Campion, now Professor of Rhetoric in the Jesuit College there. Campion's intellectual gifts would naturally attract Sidney, and we may accept the former's account that they had conversations during the latter's visit, and that Sidney put into his hands alms for distribution among the poor. But the wish was certainly father to the thought when the Jesuit spoke of the possibility of this 'poor wavering soul' being converted to Catholicism. If this took place, he truly added, it would 'astonish his noble father, the Deputy of Ireland, his uncles the Dudleys, and all the young courtiers, and Cecil himself'.

So far from leaning to Catholicism one of Sidney's earnest desires on his return journey was to meet one of the Protestant protagonists, Prince William of Orange. No such visit had been included in his original instructions, but he was pleasurably surprised to be met by a messenger with a letter from the Queen directing him to pay it. So favourable was the impression that he made on the Prince and his wife that they asked him to stand godfather to their second daughter, named Elizabeth. And he was commissioned to offer the union of the two provinces of Holland and Zeeland with the English Crown. From cryptic allusions in Languet's letters to him between June and November it would even appear that Orange offered Sidney his sister's hand in marriage, but that the tempting proposal had to be declined because it would have met with the Queen's disapproval.

By June 10th he was back in England with a greatly

enhanced reputation. Walsingham wrote enthusiastically to
Sir Henry:

> I am to impart unto you the return of the young gentle-
> man, Mr Sidney, your son, whose message very suffi-
> ciently performed, and the relating thereof, is no less
> gratefully received and well liked of her Majesty than the
> honourable opinion he hath left behind him with all the
> Princes with whom he had to negotiate hath left a most
> sweet savour and grateful remembrance of his name in
> those parts . . . There hath not been any gentleman, I am
> sure, these many years that hath gone through so honour-
> able a charge with as great commendations as he.

But the hopes for Sidney held out by such glowing words
were doomed to disappointment. His heart was set on
establishing a Protestant league, while the central aim of the
Queen's policy was to keep a balance between the power of
France and Spain. So he received no encouragement in his
cherished continental designs.

For a time his ardent mind found another subsidiary
interest. The Dudley family had been promoters of exploration from the time of the Duke of Northumberland. In
Ambrose, Earl of Warwick, Martin Frobisher had found
the patron of his voyages in search of the north-west passage
to America, and islands of gold. Towards the first of these,
in June 1576, Sidney's other uncle, the Earl of Leicester,
had contributed £150 and Philip himself £25. He had
visited the two ships, the *Michael* and the *Gabriel*, and in the
cabin of the latter had found the only six books in English
on geography and navigation, one of them dedicated to his
father and another brought out under Leicester's auspices.
On this voyage, as Sidney wrote to Languet:

> By chance, a young man, one of the ship's company,
> picked up a piece of earth which he saw glittering on the
> ground . . . this young man kept his earth by him . . . till
> his return to London. And when one of his friends saw it
> shining in an extraordinary way, he tested it and found
> that it was pure gold, unalloyed with any other metal.

Though two assayers declared it was worthless the tale of the golden ore was eagerly credited, and the Cathay Company was formed to fit out a second expedition in May 1577. The Queen herself invested £500 in it and Sidney raised his stake to £50. He even seems to have been anxious to take a personal part in the enterprise. When Frobisher returned in October he brought with him two hundred tons of the supposedly precious ore. Again the assayers declared it valueless, and once again the general public, including Sidney, clung to its belief in its worth. He subscribed £67 10s to a third expedition which set forth on May 21st 1578, when Elizabeth at Greenwich invested Frobisher with a gold chain round his neck. The expedition consisted of fifteen ships, which were to bring back two thousand tons of the ore, and were to leave behind one hundred picked men as colonists for a year. But this grandiose scheme resulted in failure, and the Cathay Company, and with it Sidney's golden dreams, ended in bankruptcy.

He was also at this time feeling further concern about the Queen's ungenerous treatment of his father, who was recalled from his post of Lord Deputy of Ireland in February 1578. His friends at Court were endeavouring unsuccessfully to procure him some mark of the Queen's favour before his return and Philip's part in these negotiations leaked out. Without justification he leapt to the conclusion that Sir Henry's secretary, Edmund Molyneux, was betraying his confidence, and on May 31st he wrote to him as follows:

> Mr Molyneux, few words are best. My letters to my father have come to the eyes of someone. Neither can I condemn any but you for it. . . . I assure you before God that if ever I know you do as much as read any letter I write to my father, without his commandment, or my consent, I will thrust my dagger into you. And trust to it, for I speak it in earnest.

This impulsive and headstrong streak in Sidney's otherwise fine nature must not be ignored. Nor were his ruffled feelings soothed later in the year by the revival of the project of a marriage between Elizabeth and the Duke d'Alençon, though this was to some degree counterbalanced by the visit to England early in 1579 of the Elector Casimir and Hubert Languet, when ties of friendship with Sidney were strengthened. Though Elizabeth was well impressed by Casimir, she persisted in her leaning towards the French matrimonial alliance, and she gave a favourable reception to Simier when he came to London as negotiator for D'Alençon. The discovery of the Earl of Leicester's secret marriage to the widowed Countess of Essex played into the Frenchman's hands, and he revealed it at once to the infuriated Queen. When D'Alençon, now the Duke of Anjou, himself arrived in August for a short visit to London, she declared, in spite of his unprepossessing appearance, that she had seen no man whom she would so willingly make her husband.

Among the very few Englishmen who were supporters of D'Alençon was Burghley's son-in-law, the Earl of Oxford. Knowing that Sidney was strongly opposed to it, he took occasion, as Fulke Greville has related, one day to order him off a tennis-court. When Sidney refused to 'be driven out with any scourge of fury', Oxford called him a puppy, and when questioned repeated the epithet a second time. Sidney gave him the lie direct, 'in respect all the world knows that puppies are gotten by dogs and children by men'. He then stalked off the court, and after hearing nothing next day sent the Earl a challenge. The Council, however, intervened to prevent a duel.

This incident had taken place within the sight and hearing of the French Commissioners, as Greville calls them. Sidney was soon to be involved in the foreign marriage question in a more direct and hazardous way. He was ordered, as he told Languet, by those whom he was bound to obey, to write a letter to the Queen, stating the reasons against the French match. They were the Leicester and Walsingham group who may have remembered his *Discourse on Ireland* and Waterhouse's encomium on it. Fully did Sidney justify their choice of him as spokesman.

He declared at once that he would set down in simple and direct terms 'the overflowing of my mind in this most important matter, purporting, as I think, the continuance of your safety, and, as I know, the joys of my life'. He warns her that the hearts of her loyal Protestant subjects will be galled, if not aliened, when they shall see you take to husband a Frenchman and a Papist in whom . . . very common people well know this, that he is the son of that Jezebel of our age, that his brother made oblation of his own sister's marriage, the easier to make massacre of our brethren in belief.

As he wrote the memory of his experience in Paris of the fatal St Bartholomew's Day flashed vividly back on Sidney's mind.

He proceeds to show how ill-qualified is 'Monsieur' to be her consort. 'His will to be as full of light ambition as is possible; besides his French disposition and his own education; his unconstant temper against his brother; his thrusting himself into the Low Country matters; his sometimes seeking the King of Spain's daughter, sometimes your Majesty, are evident testimonies of his being carried away by every wind of hope.' Here Sidney brought to bear what he had learnt on his continental diplomatic visits.

Following this up on a more personal note he suggests that if she desires marriage for 'the bliss of children', she can find this in a more suitable union than with one so much her opposite – 'He French and desirous to make France great; your Majesty English, and desirous nothing less than that France should be great.' Nor should she be influenced by the uncertainty of the succession. 'Many princes have lost their crowns, whose own children were manifest successors, and some that had their own children used as instruments of their ruin.' As for the fear of standing alone,

You must take it for a singular honour that God hath done you to be the only Protector of his Church. . . . So long as he is but Monsieur in might, and a Papist in profession, he neither can, nor will, greatly shield you; and if he get once to be King, his defence will be like Ajax's shield which rather weighed them down than defended those which bare it.

Here was an adroit appeal to Elizabeth's enthusiasm for classical literature, followed by an adjuration to let her 'excellent virtues of Piety, Justice and Liberality shine (if that indeed be possible) more and more . . . Doing as you do, you shall be as you be, the Example of Princes, the Ornament of this Age, the most excellent Fruit of your Progenitors, and the Perfect Mirror of your Posterity.'

The writing of this letter to the Queen might well count as one of the turning-points in Sidney's career. For a young man without official status to address his sovereign in such terms was, as Languet warned him, to put his own future into jeopardy. Had Elizabeth been really determined on private or public grounds, or on both, to wed D'Alençon she could have regarded her courtier's *démarche* as well-nigh treasonable and have visited it with her severe displeasure. But in spite of her shifts and turns she must have known in her inner consciousness that his protests and fears were justified, and she gave comparatively little sign of offended dignity to her audacious correspondent.

But, so far as posterity was concerned, a less obvious danger was also averted. So shrewd a judge as Elizabeth must have realized that in this gifted and courageous courtier lay a valuable potential instrument in her service. Might he not be led to follow the example of Thomas Sackville who, after the display of his literary powers in the 'Induction' to *The Mirror for Magistrates*, and, with Thomas Norton, in the tragedy of *Gorboduc*, became fully absorbed in State affairs? So might it have been with Sidney. But by good fortune he was left free to test his powers in verse and prose, for which a combination of circumstances offered unusual opportunities.

# CHAPTER VII

# 'THE LADY OF MAY' – CONNEXION WITH HARVEY AND SPENSER

Among Sidney's minor literary pieces attention is first due to the *Lady of May*, as his only effort in dramatic form, and as probably performed before Elizabeth when she visited Leicester at Wanstead in May 1578. The Queen walking in the garden with her retinue is suddenly accosted by 'one apparelled like an honest man's wife of the country', who cries for justice and presents a supplication. Her daughter 'is troubled with that notable matter which we in country call matrimony, so as I cannot choose but fear the loss of her wits, at least her honesty. Other women think they may be unhappy cumbered by one master husband, my poor daughter is oppressed with two, both loving her, both equally liked of her, both striving to deserve' her. The two rivals have brought with them their 'partakers' or partisans, and the mother begs the Queen to intervene to prevent a 'bloody controversy'. She then retires leaving with her most gracious Sovereign this supplication in verse:

> To one whose state is raised over all,
> Whose face doth oft the bravest sort enchant,
> Whose mind is such as wisest minds appal,
> Who in one self those divers gifts are plant:
> How dare I, wretch, seek there my woes to rest
> Where ears be burst, eyes dazzled, hearts oppressed.

> \* \* \*

> Your state is great, your greatness is our shield,
> Your face hurts oft, but still it doth delight;
> Your mind is wise, your wisdom makes you mild,
> God-planted gifts enrich even beggars' sight.
> So dare I, wretch, my bashful fear subdue,
> And feed mine ears, mine eyes, my heart in you.

It will be noticed that even in this dozen of incidental lines Sidney shows his partiality for verbal interlacing.

Then there came out of the woods the wooed damsel, the Lady of May, with shepherds and foresters pulling her, while she seemed to incline neither to one side or the other. 'But the Queen coming to the place where she was seen of them, though they knew not her estate, yet something there was which made them startle aside and gaze upon her', till an old shepherd Lalus stepped forward, and in affected phraseology introduces the schoolmaster Rombus 'Who can better denounce the whole foundation of the matter, although in sooth for all his loquence our young men were nothing dutious to his clerkship. Come on, come on, Master Schoolmaster, be not so bashless . . . for you can much better vent the points of it than I.'

Rombus then with many special graces made a pedantic and pompous oration, the aim of which was to display his classical learning but which was riddled with misquotations.

I am, *Potentissima Domina*, a schoolmaster, that is to say, a *Pedagogue*, one not a little versed in the disciplinating of the juvental fry, wherein (to my laud I say it) I use such geometrical proportion as neither wanted mansuetude nor correction, for so it is described, *Parcare subjectos et debellire superbo*.[1] Yet hath not the pulchritude of my virtues protected me from the contaminating hands of these plebeians, for coming *solummodo* to have parted their sanguinolent fray, they yielded me no more reverence than if I had been some *Pecorius Asinus* . . . The purity of the verity is that a certain *Pulchra puella profecto* elected and constituted by the integrated determination of all this topographical region, as the Sovereign Lady of this Dame Maia's month, hath been *quodammiono* hunted, as you would say, pursued by two, a brace, a couple, a cast of young men, to whom the crafty coward Cupid hath, *inquam*, delivered his dire-dolorous dart.

Here the Lady of May can bear with his rodomontade no longer, and cries, 'Away, away, you tedious fool!; your eyes are not worthy to look to yonder Princely sight, much less

---

[1] For *Parcere subjectis et debellare superbos.*

your foolish tongue to trouble her wise ears.' Then Rombus
'in a great chafe cries out, *O Tempori ô Moribus!* in profession
a child, in dignity a woman, in years a lady, in *caeteris* a maid,
should this turpify the reputation of my doctrine with the
superscription of a fool! *O tempori! O Moribus!*[1]

Again the May Lady bursts out, 'Leave off, good Latin
fool, and let me satisfy the long desire I have had to feed
mine eyes with the only sight this age hath granted to the
world.'

Considering that in Thomas Ashton at Shrewsbury Sidney
had had the advantage of being brought up under one
of the most progressive headmasters of the Tudor age,
one could have wished Rombus to be rather less of a figure
of fun, though he doubtless gave spice to the entertainment.
And even if Shakespeare knew of him before writing *Love's
Labour's Lost*, only in a limited degree is it true to speak of
him as 'the prototype of Holofernes'. Shakespeare's schoolmaster, like Rombus, is pedantic and 'affects the letter', but
he is not a 'Latin fool'. He talks soundly of Ovid, and cor-
rects Costard's misquotation *ad dunghill*, 'O, I smell false
Latin, "dunghill" for *unguem*.'

The May Lady kneeling before the Queen repeats more
fully what her mother has already told.

> With me have been (alas, I am ashamed to tell it) two
> young men, the one a forester named Therion, the other,
> Espilus, a shepherd, very long ever in love. Forsooth, I
> like them both and love neither. Espilus is the richer, but
> Therion the livelier. Therion doth me many pleasures
> ... but withal he grows to such rages that sometimes he
> strikes me, sometimes he rails at me. The shepherd
> Espilus, of a mild disposition, as his fortune hath not been
> to do me great service, so hath he never done me any
> wrong.

The question therefore that the May Lady has to put to the
Queen is 'whether the many deserts and many faults of
Therion, or the very small deserts and no faults of Espilus
be to be preferred'. But before she passes judgment let her
hear what either of them can say for himself in his rural

[1] For *O tempora! O Mores!*

songs. Therion begins, singing stanzas alternately with Espilus, the foresters accompanying the former on their cornets and the shepherds the latter on their recorders. The concluding stanza by Espilus runs:

Two thousand sheep I have as white as milk,
Though not so white as is thy lovely face;
The pasture rich, the wool as soft as silk,
All this I give, let me possess thy grace;
But still take heed lest thou thyself submit
To one that hath no wealth, and wants his wit.

To which Therion replies:

Two thousand deer in wildest woods I have,
Them can I take, but you I cannot hold.
He is not poor who can his freedom save;
Bound but to you, no wealth but you I would:
But take this beast, if beasts you fear to miss,
For of his beasts the greatest beast he is.

Thereupon Espilus kneeling to the Queen begs, 'Judge you to whom all Beauty's force is lent', which Therion counters with 'Judge you of Love, to whom all Love is bent.' But before she can give her verdict a contention arises between the shepherds and foresters as to which of their fellows had sung better, and as to which of their two estates was the more worshipful. Their spokesmen respectively were Dorcas, an old shepherd, and Rixus, a young forester, but somewhat unexpectedly after his previous ignominious dismissal Rombus is recalled to be 'moderator' between them. Dorcas makes a pleasantly simple plea for the pastoral life.

O sweet honey milken lambs, and is there any so flinty a heart that can find about him to speak against them that have the charge of such good souls as yon be, among whom there is no envy, and all obedience; when it is lawful for a man to be good if he list, and hath no outward cause to withdraw him from it, where the eye may be busied in considering the works of nature, and in the heart quietly rejoiced in the honest using them. If temptation, as clerks say, be the most excellent, which is so fit a life for tempters as this is, neither subject to violent oppression nor servile flattery?

Rixus admits that the shepherd's life hath some goodness, but Rombus rebukes him for not noticing Dorcas's failure in logic, 'for thus he saith that sheep are good, *ergo* the shepherd is good . . . tell him his major is a knave, his minor is a fool, and his conclusion both'. Rixus answers temperately:

> I was saying the shepherd's life had some goodness in it because it borrowed of the country quietness something like ours; but that is not all, for ours besides that quiet part doth both strengthen the body and raise up the mind with this gallant sort of activity. O sweet contemplation to see the long life of the hurtless trees, to see how in strength growing up, though never so high, they hinder not their fellows; they only enviously trouble which are crookedly bent. What is to be compared to ours where the very growing things are examples of goodness?

Rombus, for once keeping to his role of 'moderator', reminds the company that the question to be settled is whether 'the many great services and many great faults of Therion or the few small services and no faults of Espilus, be to be preferred'. Here the May Lady interrupts, 'No, no, your ordinary brains shall not deal in that matter. I have already submitted it to one whose sweet spirit hath passed through greater difficulties; neither will I that your blockheads lie in her way.' Is Sidney here making a discreet reference to some of the crises which Elizabeth had been forced to face? And it seems as if something were hidden behind the May Lady's appeal, 'vouchsafe our ears such happiness and me that particular favour as that you will judge whether of these two be more worthy of me, or whether I be worthy of them; and this I will say that in judging me, you judge more than me in it'. In any case, Sidney, while letting the Queen give her verdict in favour of Espilus, was cautious not to repeat her words or reasons which 'this paper which carrieth so base names is not worthy to contain'. The entertainment ended with a song by Espilus and a 'full consort' by the shepherds and foresters of their recorders and cornets.

In this festival show Sidney displayed sufficient command, on a slender scale, of dialogue and characterization for us to regret that he never attempted more serious dramatic work. It contained too lively echoes of his academic studies and interests with which about this period he was much occupied. If the *Lady of May* was performed when the Queen visited Leicester at Wanstead in May 1578, it was in the following July that at Audley End at Saffron Walden she was waited upon by the Vice-Chancellor of Cambridge and other University dignitaries, including Gabriel Harvey. When Harvey in commemoration of this royal occasion published his *Gratulationes Valdenses* he dedicated one section of the book in affectionate terms to Sidney. Whether the intimacy between them had begun in Cambridge, and how soon it included Edmund Spenser, is still matter for debate. Professor Wallace has pointed out that Spenser in his *A View of the Present State of Ireland* mentions that he was present at the execution of an Irish rebel in July 1577, when Sir Henry Sidney was Lord Deputy, and he may already have come into connexion with Philip, perhaps through Harvey's good offices. Ernest de Selincourt, in his Introduction to the Oxford edition of Spenser's *Poetical Works*, emphasizes the many points that they had in common. But there are few details as to the degree of their intimacy.

What has attracted special notice are the allusions in the correspondence of Spenser and Harvey to the prosodic views which they ascribe to Sidney and his friend Edward Dyer. Thus Spenser writes:

> As for the two worthy gentlemen Master Sidney and Master Dyer, they have me, I thank them, in some use of familiarity. . . . And now they have proclaimed in their ἀρειωπάγω a general surceasing and silence of bald rhymers, and also of the very best too; instead whereof they have by authority of their whole Senate prescribed certain laws and rules of quantity of English syllables for English verse, having had thereof already great practice and drawn me to their faction.

Harvey replies, 'Your new founded ἀρειωπαγων I honour more than you will or can suppose; and make greater account of the two worthy gentlemen than of two hundred Dionisy Areopagetae or the very notablest senators that ever Athens did afford of that number.'

It is still matter for debate how far these references are to be taken seriously. So far as Sidney is concerned his surviving experiments in quantitative metres are confined to some of the incidental poems in the *Arcadia*. When his true poetic genius was to find expression in *Astrophel and Stella*, it was to rank him among the 'rhymers', and 'of the very best'. And when Spenser in 1579 published his *Shepheardes Kalender*, 'containing twelve Eclogues proportionable to the twelve months, though they were in rhyming metres, he thought it well to dedicate the work to 'the noble and virtuous gentleman and worthy of all titles both of learning and chivalry, Mr Philip Sidney'.

# CHAPTER VIII

# 'THE DEFENCE OF POESIE'
## I. PHILOSOPHERS, HISTORIANS AND POETS

It was for the dedication in the same year of another very different work to 'the right noble gentleman, Master Philip Sidney, Esquire', that posterity, though not Sidney, has to be thankful. Stephen Gosson, born in 1554, had passed from Corpus Christi College, Oxford, to London where, according to Francis Meres, he won a reputation as a pastoral poet. He also tried his hand at the stage with three plays of different types, *Catiline's Conspiracy*, doubtless a tragedy; *Captain Morio*, 'a cast of Italian devices', and *Praise at Parting*, a morality. Whether through lack of success or backbitings of conscience, he turned against the theatre, and not only against the drama but against the poetic art in all its forms. He set forth his views after his conversion in a treatise entitled *The School of Abuse*, containing 'a pleasant invective against Poets, Pipers, Players, Jesters, and such like caterpillers of a commonwealth . . . A discussion as pleasant for gentlemen that favour learning as profitable for all that will follow virtue'.

Gosson may have thought that Sidney was not only a champion of Protestantism in its political aspects but that he had a Puritan antipathy to the arts. If so he was speedily undeceived. 'New books', wrote Spenser (to Gabriel Harvey on October 15th, 1579), 'I hear of none but only of one that writing a certain book called the *School of Abuse*, and dedicating it to Master Sidney, was for his labour scorned, if at least it be in the goodness of that nature to scorn.' As Sidney's *Defence of Poesie* was not published till 1595 its date is uncertain, and Spenser may not have been referring to it. But there can be no doubt that in writing his treatise, Sidney, though he does not name him, was replying to the Philistine challenger who by his dedication had so brazenly claimed him as an ally.

The work was entered for the first time under the title

of 'A treatise in commendation of Poetrie or the Defence of Poesy' in the Register of the Stationers' Company on November 29th, 1594, by William Ponsonby, and was published by him as *The Defence of Poesie* in the following year. On April 12th, 1595, it was re-entered by Henry Olney, under an agreement with Ponsonby, securing his rights, with the title 'An Apologie for Poetrie', and so published. In a flamboyant epistle to the Reader, Olney claims that 'The stormy Winter . . . which hath so long held back the glorious Sunshine of divine Poesy is here by the sacred pen-breathing words of divine Sir Philip Sidney . . . for ever banished eternity.' For the 1598 folio the Countess of Pembroke chose Ponsonby's issue.

It is characteristic of the unconventional elements in Sidney's *Defence* that he begins with a reminiscence of his sojourn at the Emperor Maximilian II's Court in Vienna, in the winter of 1574–5, when he and the Resident, Edward Wotton, were being trained in the courtly accomplishment of horsemanship by the equerry, John Pietro Pugliano. He claimed that 'soldiers were the noblest estate of mankind, and horsemen the noblest of soldiers', adding 'what a peer-less beast a horse was'. So that, as Sidney says in a charmingly sly aside, 'if I had not been a piece of a logician before I came to him, I think he would have persuaded me to have wished myself a horse'.

Following Pugliano's example Sidney declares, 'I will give you a nearer example of myself, who (I know not by what mischance) in these my not old years and idlest times, having slipt into the title of a Poet, am provoked to say something unto you in the defence of that my unelected vocation.'

From what has been already said, it is evident that Sidney is here belittling his own poetic achievement. On the other hand, it has been urged against the originality of his *Defence* that he has drawn many of his arguments and illustrations from classical writers or Renaissance humanists like Minturno and Scaliger. While this is true, Sidney expresses himself in such idiomatic and forcible English that his work has its own distinctive stamp, and in essentials retains its significance throughout the centuries.

His first claim for poetry is its antiquity. Those who defame it are ungrateful to 'that which, in the noblest nations and languages that are known, hath been the first light giver to ignorance, and the first nurse, whose milk by little and little enabled them to feed afterwards of tougher know-ledges'. He quotes examples from Greece and Rome, and continues, 'So in the Italian language the first that made it aspire to be a treasure-house of science were the poets, Dante, Boccaccio and Petrarch. So in our English were Gower and Chaucer.' How pat it would have been to Sidney's purpose could he have instanced *Beowulf* and Cynewulf!

The second claim for poetry is its universality. All nations have 'some feeling' of it. Here Sidney seems to be drawing partly on his authorities, partly on personal contacts.

> In Turkey, besides their law-giving divines they have no other writers but poets. In our neighbour country, Ireland, where truly learning goeth very bare, yet are their poets held in a devout reverence. Even among the most barbarous and simple Indians, where no writing is, yet have they their poets who make and sing songs, which they call *Areytlos*, both of their ancestors' deeds and praises of their Gods . . . In Wales, the true remnant of the ancient Britons, as there are good authorities to show the long time they had poets, which they called *Bards*, so through all the conquests of Romans, Saxons, Danes and Normans, . . . yet do their poets, even to this day, last.

After making some play with the Latin name for a poet *Vates* (Diviner, fore-seer, prophet) and the Greek *Poietes* (Maker), Sidney proceeds to the core of his *Defence*. All arts, he de-clares, are chiefly concerned with the works of nature, but their various practitioners, of whom he gives a list, deal only with particular aspects of it.

> Only the poet . . . , lifted up with the vigour of his own invention, doth grow in effect another nature, in making things either better than Nature bringeth forth or quite anew . . . Nature never set forth the earth in so rich tapestry as divers poets have done, neither with pleasant rivers, fruitful trees, sweet-smelling flowers, nor whatso-

ever else may make the too much loved earth more lovely.
Her world is brazen, the poets only deliver a golden.

After this memorable last sentence Sidney claims that so it
is with man himself where poetry presents superhuman
paragons, not to be less esteemed because they are fictitious,
'for any understanding knoweth the skill of the artificer
standeth in that *Idea* or fore-conceipt of the work, and not
in the work itself. And that the poet hath that *Idea* is manifest by delivering them forth in such excellency as he hath
imagined them'.

The use of *Idea* here seems to spring, directly or otherwise, from a Platonic source, and it is followed by another
debt, again perhaps at second hand, to Hellenism. 'Poesty
therefore is an art of imitation, for so Aristotle termeth it in
his word *Mimesis*, that is to say, a representing, counterfeiting or figuring forth; to speak metaphorically, a speaking
picture: with this end, to teach and delight.' These last
words are expanded and stressed in a later passage where
poets are said to

> merely make, to imitate, and imitate both to delight and
> teach; and delight, to move men to take that goodness in
> hand, which without delight they would fly as from a
> stranger; and teach, to make them know that goodness
> whereunto they are moved.

Sidney, it is true, here recognizes the element of 'delight',
the *dulce* in poetry, but it is primarily as a handmaid to the
*utile*, the didactic function. He thus shares in the tendency
of Renaissance critics to over-emphasize the directly edifying
aims and effects of poetry, which led Milton towards the
close of the period to speak of Spenser as a better teacher
than Scotus or Aquinas. And this concern with the function
of poetry rather than with its form is accountable for what
is the most heterodox and disputable thesis in the *Defence*,
that verse is 'but an ornament and no cause to poetry, sith
there have been many most excellent poets that never versi-
fied, and now swarm many versifiers that need never answer
to the name of poets'. As examples of poets who have written
in prose Sidney cites Xenophon whose portraiture of Cyrus

is an 'absolute heroical poem', and Heliodorus 'in his sugared invention of that picture of love in *Theagines and Chariclea*'. This, in his opinion, proves that 'it is not rhyming and versing that maketh a poet. But it is that feigning notable images of virtues, vices, or what else, with that delightful teaching, which must be the right describing note to know a poet by.'

Here again Sidney takes as the criterion of poetry not its form but its didactic content. He ignores the distinction between verse, with its recurring beats, whether in traditional moulds or in the freer forms that have been recently sponsored, and the essentially more flexible rhythm of prose. It only creates confusion if even the most highly imaginative and decorative prose is brought within the poetic classification. And Sidney himself partly qualifies his statement by admitting that 'the Senate of poets hath chosen verse as their fittest raiment . . . not speaking (table-talk fashion or like men in a dream) words as they chanceably fall from the mouth, but each syllable of each word by just proportion according to the dignity of the subject'. How forcible a description of a poet's endeavour to find perfect expression!

Sidney himself reaches the peak of his exposition in the pages that follow, wherein his critical insight, fortified by his studies as a 'clerk of Oxenford', is blended with his lively humour and dramatic sense. The highest end of all knowledge, he avers, called by the Greeks *Architecktonice*, is the knowledge of a man's self, 'with the end of well doing and not of well knowing only'. The first who claim to impart this are the moral philosophers,

> whom, me thinketh, I see coming towards me with a sullen gravity, as though they could not abide vice by daylight, rudely clothed for to witness outwardly their contempt of outward things, with books in their hands against glory, whereto they set their names . . . these men casting largesse as they go of Definitions, Divisions and Distinctions, with a scornful interrogative do soberly ask whether it be possible to find any path so ready to lead a man to virtue as that which teaches what virtue is.

The moral philosophers further assert that they make known

virtue's 'enemy vice, which must be destroyed, and his cumbersome servant passion, which must be mastered'; and that they extend the application of their teaching from the individual to the family and the State. Here, however, there is a dramatic interruption.

The historian scarcely giveth leisure to the moralist, to say so much but that he, loaden with old mouse-eaten records, authorizing himself (for the most part) upon other histories, whose greatest authorities are built upon the notable foundation of hear-say, having much ado to accord differing writers and to pick truth out of partiality . . . denieth, in a great chafe, that any man for teaching of virtue, and virtuous actions, is comparable to him. 'The philosopher' saith he 'teacheth a disputative virtue but I do an active; his virtue is excellent in the dangerless academy of Plato, but mine showeth forth her honourable face in the battles of Marathon, Pharsalia, Poictiers and Agincourt.'

Sidney here, more entertainingly than impartially, fastens on the weaker side of the English chroniclers of his day in accepting legendary traditions, like London being New Troy, as verified fact. But apart from this playful mockery he establishes his contention that the philosopher teaches by precept, the historian by example. 'But both not having both, do both halt. . . . Now doth the peerless poet perform both, for whatsoever the philosopher sayeth should be done, he giveth a perfect picture of it in some men, by whom he presupposeth it was done. So as he completes the general notion with the particular example.' The instances that he gives are more striking in their variety than entirely cogent today. They range from the Scriptural parables of Dives and Lazarus and the Prodigal Son, and the Greek heroes in Homer and Sophocles, to Aesop's fables, Chaucer's Pandarus and the pattern of a perfect commonwealth in More's *Utopia*.

But where Sidney rises to the full height of his argument and establishes, as I think, the claim of his *Defence* to be a Classic in its field is in his realization of the predominance of imaginative over historical truth. Here he proves himself in a fuller degree than any previous Englishman to be an understanding disciple of Aristotle.

> But now may it be alleged that if this imagining of matters be so fit for the imagination, then must the historian needs surpass, who bringeth you images of true matters, such as indeed were done, and not such as fantastically or falsely may be suggested to have been done. Truly, Aristotle himself, in his discourse of Poesie, plainly determineth this question, saying that poetry is *philosophoteron* and *spoudaioteron*, that is to say, it is more philosophical and more studiously serious than history. His reason is because poesie dealeth with *Katholon*, that is to say, with the universal consideration; and the history with *Kathekaston*, the particular . . . Thus far Aristotle, which reason of his (as all his) is most full of reason.

Sidney follows this up with a number of illustrative examples, taken almost entirely from classical texts on the one hand, and from ancient history on the other, to prove that the poet is the Monarch among the followers of the arts. But for those to whom these make little appeal there is the persuasive note sounded in the *vox humana* of an exquisitely rounded sentence.

> He beginneth not with obscure definitions, which must blur the margent with interpretations and load the memory with doubtfulness; but he cometh to you with words set in delightful proportion, either accompanied with, or prepared for, the well enchanting skill of music; and with a tale forsooth he cometh unto you, with a tale which holdeth children from play, and old men from the chimney corner.

From these general considerations Sidney then turns to a brief defence of some of the chief poetic types, the pastoral, the elegy, satire, comedy, tragedy, the lyric, the heroical or epic. A few points stand out. Sidney makes too much of the moral effect of comedy when he claims that it represents the common errors of our life 'in the most ridiculous and scornful sort that may be; so as it is impossible that any beholder can be content to be such a one'. He prevails more with his advocacy of the lyric, where again he strikes one of his affecting personal notes. 'I never heard the old song of Percy and Douglas that I found not my heart moved more than with a trumpet, and yet it is sung but by some blind crowder with no rougher voice than rude style.'[1] And there is a yet more homely touch when he compares the 'poet-whippers' who find fault even with the heroical, 'the best and most accomplished kind of poetry' to 'some good women, who often are sick but in faith they cannot tell where'.

At this point Sidney briefly recapitulates the main heads of his defence on its broader issues and turns, as it were, aside to answer some of the objections of Gosson and other *misomousoi* – or poet-haters. They assert that a man might better spend his time in 'more fruitful knowledges', but this is merely a case of *petere principium*. Secondly, that poetry is the mother of lies, but the poet affirms nothing and therefore never lieth. Thirdly, that it is the nurse of abuse, 'infecting us with many pestilent desires', but granting all this, it is not that 'poetry abuseth man's wit, but that man's wit abuseth poetry'. Lastly, that Plato banished poets out of his commonwealth, but this was because of their abuse of poetry, by filling 'the world with wrong opinions of the Gods'. In his dialogue *Ion* he gives high honour to poetry, and thus is a patron, not an adversary, of its lovers.

[1] See p. 17.

# CHAPTER IX

# 'THE DEFENCE OF POESIE'
## II – CRITICISM OF CONTEMPORARY DRAMA

Sidney would have done well, in his own phrase, to have here given his pen a full stop, and not appended to the critical analysis of his main treatise a pessimistic survey of the state of English letters. It is true that he was writing, whatever may be the exact date, just at the dawn of the great Elizabethan literary period, and that he has praise for the *Mirror for Magistrates*, for the Earl of Surrey's Lyrics, and, with reservation, for Spenser's *The Shepheardes Calender*. But he ignores *Tottel's Miscellany*, including much of Sir Thomas Wyatt's notable verse, and the *Posies* of George Gascoigne.

But it is when he turns to drama that he becomes liable to some of the reproofs that he had addressed to the scornful critics of poetry. Here his Classical and Renaissance schooling which had stood him in such good stead in the philosophical sections of the *Defence* led him astray. Except for *Gorboduc*, Sackville and Norton's tragedy, he has no good word for any plays that he has seen, which observe 'rules neither of honest civility nor of skilful poetry'. Though the schools, the universities, the Inns of Court and the popular stages had produced, especially in the fields of comedy and moral interlude, plays of considerable merit between 1550 and 1580, Sidney could have seen few of them performed, and in any case they would not have conformed to his perverted standard. He was misled by the Italian humanists who had fathered upon Aristotle, rightly concerned only with unity of action, the two fictitious unities of place and time. In these respects even *Gorboduc* had fallen short of the exact tragic model. 'For where the stage should always represent but one place, and the uttermost time presupposed in it should be, both by Aristotle's precept and common reason, but one day, there is both many days, and many places artificially imagined.'

And from his almost sorrowful indictment of the lapses in

*Gorboduc* Sidney changes to a bantering tone in making mock of what he considers to be the absurdities in the generality of contemporary plays.

> Where you shall have Asia on the one side, and Africk on the other, and so many other under-Kingdoms, that the player when he cometh in, must ever begin with telling where he is, or else the tale will not be conceived. Now ye shall have three ladies walk to gather flowers, and then we must believe the stage to be a garden. By and by, we have news of shipwreck in the same place, and then we are to blame if we accept it not for a rock. Upon the back of that comes out a hideous monster, with fire and smoke, and then the miserable beholders are bound to take it for a cave. While in the meantime two armies fly in, represented with four swords and bucklers, and then what hard heart will not receive it for a pitched field?
>
> Now of time they are much more liberal, for ordinary it is that two young Princes fall in love. After many traverses, she is got with child, delivered of a fair boy; he is lost, groweth a man, falls in love, and is ready to get another child; and all this in two hours' space: which how absurd it is in sense even sense may imagine, and art hath taught, and all ancient examples justified.

Of course when the earliest primitive London theatres were only beginning to supplement or take the place of stages in the court-yards of inns or the halls of private houses, some of Sidney's shafts go home. Even some twenty years later Shakespeare in *Henry V* at the Curtain or the Globe has to ask pardon for his attempt to cram

> Within this wooden O the very casques
> That did affright the air at Agincourt.

And in *Pericles* Gower has to appear as Chorus to bridge over the intervals of time in the action.

An additional charge by Sidney is that the contemporary plays are 'neither right tragedies nor right comedies, mingling Kings and clowns, not because the matter so carrieth it, but thrust in clowns by head and shoulders to play a part in majestical matters, with neither decency nor discretion'.

Was not Hamlet, speaking here for Shakespeare, to warn the actors at Elsinore? 'Let those that play your clowns speak no more than is set down for them; for there be of them that will themselves laugh, to set on some quantity of barren spectators to laugh too, though, in the meantime, some necessary question of the play be then to be considered.'

Where Sidney fails to be convincing in this section of his treatise is not in his indictment of the weaknesses of contemporary plays, even if he stressed these to the exclusion of their better elements. The capital charge against him is that instead of giving the dramatist experimental freedom of plan, in accordance with his individual instinct and vision, he sought to bind him to a predetermined pattern, an 'exact model'. It was an irony of fortune that before the *Defence* was to appear in print Lyly, Kyd, Marlowe and the youthful Shakespeare were to invalidate Sidney's special pleading, and to endow the English theatre with novel and inspiring dramatic types.

Sidney takes leave of 'this play matter', as he calls it, with the almost petulant gesture of having 'lavished out too many words on it'. But this is because it lends itself specially to abuse, or, in another of his homely images, 'like an unmannerly daughter, showing a bad education, causeth her mother Poesy's honesty to be called in question'.

The remaining few pages of the *Defence* deal chiefly with technical matters, diction, alliteration, similes, grammar, quantitative and accented rhymed verse. In discussing these Sidney adopts a truly patriotic attitude. To those who depreciate English as a 'mingled language' he retorts that it is so much the better for taking the best from its different sources. Another of its advantages is its lack of 'those cumbersome differences of cases, genders, moods and tenses, which I think was a piece of the Tower of Babylon's curse'. Without pronouncing on the comparative merits of classical quantative and modern accented rhymed verse, Sidney claims, in a comparison of English with the other vulgar tongues, that it is fittest for both forms. Similarly in its variety of rhymes, single, double and treble, it excels its rivals. Whether or not prosodists today would support all Sidney's claims for English as the outstanding poetic medium, it is to his credit that he had given serious attention to the technical aspects of his inquiry. He brings it to a close by adjuring all those who have had 'the evil luck to read this ink-wasting toy of mine, even in the name of the nine Muses, no more to scorn the sacred mysteries of poesy'. If they turn a deaf ear, they must endure the curse, 'that while you live, you live in love and never get favour for lacking skill of a sonnet; and when you die, your memory dies from the earth for want of an epitaph'.

Thus Sidney who had begun the *Defence* with an anecdote about horsemanship ends it on a playfully threatening note. It is the combination of such features of an informal *causerie* with the critical insight into the fundamental issues in debate between himself and his opponents that gives his treatise a unique quality. If, after the fashion of his period, he has made too much of the didactic value of poetry, and if he has proved to be short-sighted in his estimate of contemporary, especially dramatic, verse, these failings are for overweighted by his philosophic grasp of the essentials at stake, the width, if not the depth, of his linguistic scholarship, and the flexible grace of his style. We can apply to his treatise his own favourite formula about the poetic art that it can both teach and delight.

# CHAPTER X

# THE OLD 'ARCADIA' – MANUSCRIPTS – FIRST PRINTED VERSION

But during a considerable period of detachment from Court and political affairs Sidney did not find a treatise on poetry sufficient to occupy his whole time and interest. He had always been in close intimacy with his sister Mary, who after her appearance at Court at Elizabeth's invitation in 1575 soon became a reigning beauty. In her fifteenth year she attracted the attention of the widowed second Earl of Pembroke, aged forty, a friend of her uncle, the Earl of Leicester, who informed her father of the likelihood of a match between them. In spite of the disparity in age between the pair, Sir Henry replied 'protesting before the Almighty God that if He and all the powers on earth would give me choice for a husband for her I would choose the Earl of Pembroke'. The difficulty, however, was to find the £3,000 which Pembroke had stipulated as his bride's marriage portion. It was paid in instalments of which the last was on February 3rd, 1578. After the wedding on April 21st, Sidney spent much of his leisure time at the Pembrokes' country seat Wilton. It was amidst these pastoral surroundings and at the request of the Countess that Sidney, as he tells in the letter prefaced to the first printed edition, in 1590, began his romance the *Arcadia*. He states that it was written on loose sheets of paper, most of it in her presence, the rest on sheets sent to her as fast as they were written. It was done only for her, only to her. She is to keep it to herself, 'or to such friends as will weigh errors in the balance of good will'.

These last words seem to be almost echoed in a note which Edmund Molyneux, Sir Henry Sidney's secretary in Ireland, contributed to Stow's continuation of Holinshed's *Chronicle*, Vol. III, f. 1554a, and which first mentions the *Arcadia* by name. Between Sidney's return from his embassy to Germany and his further royal employment, at his vacant and spare times of leisure (for he could endure at no time to be idle and void of action) he made his book which he named *Arcadia* . . . few works of like subject hath been either of some more earnestly sought, choicely kept, nor placed in better place, and amongst better jewels than that was, so that a special dear friend he should be that could once obtain a copy of it.

But it is only within recent years that it has been recognized that the copies of which Molyneux here speaks and the printed 1590 edition of the romance represent different versions of the *Arcadia*. Yet a clue had been provided by a letter of Fulke Greville to Sir Francis Walsingham, Sidney's father-in-law, endorsed November 1586, soon after his death.

Sir, this day one Ponsonby a book-binder in Paul's Churchyard, came to me and told me that there was one in hand to print Sir Philip Sidney's old *Arcadia*, asking me if it were done with your honour's voice or any other of his friends. I told him to my knowledge, no; then he advised me to give warning of it, either to the Archbishop or Doctor Cousin, who have, as he says, a copy to peruse to that end.

Sir, I am loth to renew his memory unto you, but yet in this I must presume, for I have sent my lady, your daughter, at her request, a correction of that old one, done four or five years since, which he left in trust with me, whereof there is no more copies, and fitter to be printed than the first, which is so common: notwithstanding, even that to be amended by a direction set down under his own hand, how and why, so as in many respects, especially the care of printing of it, is to be done with more deliberation.

This letter is valuably informative in various ways. It proves that a copy of what Greville calls 'the old *Arcadia*', and what Molyneux praises so highly, had come into the possession of a publisher, who was about to apply to the Archbishop of Canterbury or Dr Cousin[1] for a licence to print it. But for the intervention of William Ponsonby and

[1] Richard Cosin, Dean of Arches, authorized by the Archbishop to license the printing of books.

of Greville, the *Arcadia* in its original form would, it appears, have been given to the reading public in 1586 or 1587. No licence was now forthcoming till August 23rd, 1588, when it was issued to Ponsonby himself. And there was further delay till 1590, when the book appeared in quarto – not the old *Arcadia* but the newer version. Greville must have furnished Ponsonby with his unique copy of this, which he had submitted to Sidney's widow for her approval, and which contained further autograph directions for additional amendments. A manuscript copy of the old *Arcadia* must have been seen by Abraham Fraunce who, in his *Arcadian Rhetorick* (1588), included about eighty quotations from the original version. But as soon as printed texts appeared they naturally held the field. Thereafter there were only a few references to 'the first *Arcadia*' by Sir John Harington in a note to his translation of *Orlando Furioso* (1591), and in the 1613 edition to 'that first written *Arcadia* of his which only passed from hand to hand and was never printed'.

Afterwards for nearly three centuries the existence of 'that first written *Arcadia*' was forgotten. It was not till 1907 that the antiquarian bookseller Bertram Dobell bought in a London auction room a manuscript copy of the *Arcadia* which was found to represent a version differing from the printed text. From Dobell it passed into the hands of the New York book auctioneers, Dodd, Mead & Co, who sold it to the collector, Mr W. A. White. Among the names scribbled in it, presumably of previous owners, are those of several members of the Clifford family, and it is thus cited as the Clifford MS.

Soon afterwards Dobell was fortunate enough to secure two other manuscripts of the old *Arcadia*. One of these had been in the library of the Earl of Ashburnham, and was sold by Sotheby late in 1907 for £70 to W. A. White, from whom it passed to the Huntington library in San Marino, California. The other had been mentioned in the sale catalogue of Thomas Thorpe in 1836 and had been bought by Sir Thomas Phillips. It was included in the sale of part of his library by Sotheby in June 1908, though there was no indication of its special character. This again was left for recognition by Bertram Dobell, who gave £119 for it.

In the *Quarterly Review*, July 1909, in an article truly entitled 'New Light upon Sir Philip Sidney's *Arcadia*', Dobell gave an account of his purchases and their significance. One result was that when he put up the Phillips' MS. again for sale, the British Museum in March 1914 gave £185 for it (Add. MS., 38,892). Since then the British Museum has acquired by presentation in 1926 another manuscript of the old version, which belonged to Miss M. E. Davies (Add. MS., 41,204).

Two other manuscripts have now been identified at Oxford. One of them is the Bodleian (MS. é Mus. 37. Folio: ff. 1 + 247), which was apparently acquired between 1655 and 1660. According to Professor R. W. Zandvoort it presents the best text of the old *Arcadia*.

On the other hand a manuscript in Queen's College library (L.301. Codex chartaceus, in folio ff. 138 sec, XVII) is the most faulty, though it contains after the last eclogue in the first Book a passage dealing with the problem of rhymed accented *versus* rhymeless quantitative metre which, as has been seen, was one of Sidney's interests at this time.

It was almost twenty years after Dobell's discovery of the Clifford MS. before the old *Arcadia* became accessible in print. In 1926 Professor Albert Feuillerat of the University of Rennes added it as Volume IV to his edition of *The Complete Works of Sir Philip Sidney*, published by the Cambridge University Press. Feuillerat gave his reasons for choosing the Clifford MS. from which to set up his text. It is a large quarto carefully written in a sixteenth-century English hand. It is in a beautiful state of preservation. Being in a private New York library it is practically inaccessible to European scholars, though Mr White gave Professor Feuillerat every facility for his editorial work. This included a list of errors in the manuscript which have been corrected, a series of notes, and a detailed table showing the relation between the old *Arcadia* and the 1590–3 *Arcadia*.

In his prefatory note Feuillerat mentioned R. W. Zandvoort of Nimeguen as engaged in a study of Sidney as a thinker. In 1929 Zandvoort covered a somewhat wider field in his volume published at Amsterdam, *Sidney's 'Arcadia'. A comparison between the two versions*. This began with a comparison of part of the text of the manuscripts and that of the early printed editions.

All this is of high scholarly interest and value. But in my general study of Sidney in his various aspects my attempt is to compare the old *Arcadia* in its broader features with the revised version, and to assess their respective merits.

# CHAPTER XI

# THE OLD 'ARCADIA' – ORACLES AND SEX ENTANGLEMENTS

I would first draw attention to the heading in the manuscripts of each of the five sections as the first, second, etc., 'Book or Act', followed by the Eclogues. Thus Sidney, while writing a romance, has also a dramatic model before him, and, as will be seen, much of the dialogue might be lifted straight into a play. The first sentence transports us into the scenic background of all that is to follow.

> Arcadia among the provinces of Greece was ever had in singular reputation partly for the sweetness of the air and other natural benefits, but principally for the moderate and well-tempered minds of the people.

Its ruler was a mighty Duke named Basilius, Prince of sufficient skill to govern so quiet a country. His wife was Gynecia, the daughter of the King of Cyprus, 'a lady worthy enough to have had the name in continual remembrance, if her later time had not blotted her well governed youth'. Were these enigmatic words intended to excite the Countess of Pembroke from the beginning? At any rate they prove that Sidney already had thought out the main lines of his singular plot which starts from the riddling reply of the Delphic Oracle to Basilius 'desirous to know the certainty of things to come, wherein there is nothing so certain as our continual uncertainty'. Concerning his daughters Pamela, just seventeen, and Philoclea, her junior by a year, he is told:

> Thy elder care shall from thy careful face
> By princely means be stolen and yet not lost.
> The younger shall with Nature's bliss embrace
> An uncouth love which Nature hateth most.

And the Oracle adds:

> Thou with thy wife adultery shall commit,
> And in thy throne a foreign State shall sit,
> All this on thee this fatal year shall hit.

In the hope of defeating these menacing prophecies Basilius decides to appoint his counseller Philanax as ruler in his place for the fatal year, and retires to a solitary place where there are two lodges. In the one he dwells with his wife and his younger daughter, Philoclea, 'the beauty of the world'. In the other he places the elder, Pamela, with his herdsman Dametas, and his wife Miso and his daughter Mopsa. He thought that in this way he would secure her against any mishap of princely origin. But it is a fundamental principle in romance that whoever seeks to frustrate an oracle hastens its fulfilment.

So it now happens with Basilius. Fate had brought to the neighbourhood of the lodges two wandering princes, Pyrocles, son to Euarchus, King of Macedon, and his cousin – german Musidorus, Duke of Thessalia, 'both like in virtues, near in years, near in blood, but nearest of all in friendship'. It is noteworthy that Sidney here deliberately refuses to complicate the story by relating their adventures *en route* to Arcadia. 'What befell unto them, what valiant acts they did, passing in one year's space through the lesser Asia, Syria and Egypt; how many ladies they defended from wrongs and disinherited persons restored to their rights, it is a work for a higher style than mine.'

Sidney's story thus begins in the house of Kerxenes, a principal gentleman of Martinea, where the two princes become at first resident. Here Pyrocles falls in love with Philoclea, seen in a picture with her parents. He resolves to adopt the disguise of an Amazon named Cleophila to get access to her. Musidorus attempts to dissuade him from this effeminate love of a woman which 'doth so womanish a man that if you yield to it, it will not only make you a famous Amazon but a launder,[1] a distaff-spinner or whatever other vile occupation their idle heads can imagine or their weak hands perform'. A too prolonged sentimental debate follows. At last, however, Musidorus is overcome by the strength of his cousin's passion and offers his help to array him in Amazonian attire, the gorgeous details of which should be marked by all students of Elizabethan costume. 'Sweet cousin,' exclaims Musidorus, 'since you are framed of such

[1] Laundress.

loving metal, I pray you take heed of looking yourself in a
glass, lest Narcissus' fortune fall unto you.'

The princely pair take leave of their host in Mantinea to
be near the lonely lodges, and here the singing voice of
Cleophila (as Pyrocles must now be called) wakes the shepherd Dametas, 'a short, lean fellow, of black hair and notably
backed, for a burden, one of his eyes out'. His splay-footed
wife Miso observed *decorum* by having in a wretched body
a froward mind, and their daughter Mopsa was 'a fit woman
to participate of both their perfections'. Dametas comes to
the place where he had heard Cleophila singing, and swears
with a voice 'like him that plays Hercules in a play and God
knows never had Hercules' fancy in his head'. What an
anticipation of Bottom's 'I could play Ercles rarely or a part
to tear a cat in'! And when Cleophila, instead of answering,
fetches a deep sigh, Dametas forestalls a higher Jack in
office, Dogberry. 'Thou woman or boy, or both, or whatsoever you be, I tell thee there is no place for thee; get thee
gone. I tell thee it is the Duke's pleasure, I tell thee it is Mr
Dametas' pleasure . . . I tell thee I am the Duke's officer
and have the charge of him and his daughters.' When she
takes no notice of him, he hits her with the blunt end of his
billhook, crying 'Maid Marian, am not I a person to be
answered?' But when the supposed maid lays hand upon her
sword, he rushes off to the Duke's lodge, where the door is
opened by Philoclea. Without making a reverential bow he
'commanded her in the Duke's name, she should tell the
Duke he was to speak with the Duke, for he, forsooth, had
things to tell the Duke which pertained to the Duke's service'. Basilius bids him bring him into the presence of the
Amazon with whom he at once begins to fall in love. To
persuade her to stay with him he sends for his wife and
daughters. The flesh-and-blood Philoclea proves to be even
more enchanting than her picture, and Cleophila willingly
surrenders to her plea that she should remain with them.

Meanwhile Musidorus hiding in a grove was a witness of
what befell his transformed friend, and would often say to
himself, 'O sweet Pyrocles, how art thou bewitched! Where
is thy virtue – where is the use of thy reason? How much
am I inferior unto thee in all the powers of the mind, and

yet know I that all the heavens cannot bring me to such a thraldom.'

The words were scarcely spoken than the sight of Pamela's beauty struck him with so violent a love that he ran away through the grove like a madman. Meeting with a shepherd, Menalcas, in festival array to take part in an entertainment before the Duke, he exchanged garments with him in order to have access to Pamela. Thus apparelled, and singing a doleful ditty, he is found by his 'he she friend', Cleophila, who rallies him upon his astonishing change of view. This culminates in Musidorus calling himself Dorus and the younger brother of a shepherd recently dead, and bribing Dametas with a large sum of gold to let him enter his service. Fortune favours the lovers for a pastoral entertainment in a fair meadow is suddenly interrupted by the onset of a fierce lion and bear, who put the shepherds to flight. But Cleophila saves Philoclea from the lion, whose head he cuts off and presents to her, though he has been severely wounded.

All this is seen by Gynecia, whose heart was possessed with a new wonderful passionate love of Cleophila, at the first sight of whom 'her heart gave her she was a man, thus for some strange cause disguised, which now in effect this combat did assure her of, because she measured the possibility of all women's hearts out of her own'. They are soon joined by Pamela, having in her hand the paw of the bear which Dorus had killed with his shepherd's knife, after she had fainted with fear, and Dametas had taken shelter in a bush.

Thus the tangle of loves arising out of the confusions of sex is completed. This had an irresistible fascination for the Elizabethans which we find it difficult to appreciate today. On the stage it had its origin and partial justification in the acting of women's parts by boys. But in the long-drawn-out narrative of a romance, even Sidney's skill and delicacy of touch find it difficult to make the equivical 'he she' situation fully palatable.

It is further developed in Book II, where on the next morning Gynecia astonishes Cleophila by revealing that she has discovered the secret of her sex and begs 'take pity on

me, O Cleophila, but not as Cleophila, and disguise not
with me in words, as I know thou doest in apparel'. They are
interrupted by Basilius who further amazes Cleophila by an
amorous declaration. Thus while still unknown to Philoclea
the pretended Amazon is exposed to 'the doting love of
Basilius and the violent passion of Gynecia'. Dorus meanwhile was also in a quandary for he found that in his disguise
he could not be accounted by Pamela as more than a good
servant. So he hit upon the ruse of counterfeiting violent
love to Mopsa, which attracted the attention of Pamela, as
implying either great ignorance or a hidden meaning. So
extravagant are the terms which he uses that Mopsa can
only reply, 'In faith you jest with me, you are a merry man
indeed.' But they prepare the way for Dorus under a feigned
tale to reveal to Pamela his adventures and his real station.

Then returning to Philoclea, Sidney describes her troubles
with baffling emotion, visiting by moonlight a forest glade,
where she voices and sings her woe. Her father, rejected by
Cleophila, to whom he has declared his passion, commissions
Philoclea to plead for him and thus short-sightedly gives her
lover the long-sought opportunity of disclosing himself and
his passion. 'O, only Princess, attend here a miserable
miracle of affection. Behold here before your eyes Pyrocles,
Prince of Macedon, whom only you have brought to this
fall of fortune and unused metamorphosis, whom you only
have made neglect his country, forget his father and lastly
forsake himself.' Philoclea, after a short inward struggle,
confessed, 'thou hast then the victory, use it with virtue',
and with many embracings, 'as it seemed their souls desired
to meet . . . they passed the promise of marriage'. At this
climax of their bliss Gynecia suddenly appears and in her
jealous rage bids Philoclea go home and keep company with
her lonely father.

It may now have occurred to Sidney that there was a
danger of even the Countess of Pembroke being cloyed with
a surfeit of amorous entanglements, and he suddenly diver-
sifies his tale with a semi-political episode. There breaks
upon the air the confused medley of voices of a mutinous
multitude. This tumult was the outcome of a banquet held
in celebration of the Duke's birthday in a village called

Phagona near the two lodges. Here a number of the villagers heated with wine began to make the Duke's person their table-talk, and they descended to a direct dislike of his living away from them. Finally their prayers for him turned to threatenings, and 'the solemnizing his birthday tended to the cause of his funeral. For arming themselves with anything that came handy the rebels advanced with murderous intent, driving before them Philoclea and Gynecia, who are rescued by another display of Cleophila's valour, aided by Basilius and by Dorus, when he is satisfied that Pamela is safe in a cave with the Dametas family. But above all it is an eloquent oration by Cleophila that restores loyalty and order.

O what would the first Arcadians, your worthy predecessors, say if they lived at this time and saw their offspring defaming such an excellent Monarchy, which they with much labour and blood wisely established? No, no, your honest hearts will never so gratify your hateful neighbours, nor degenerate from your famous ancestors.

A promise by Cleophila of amnesty to all who would turn their weapons against those who still threatened the Duke's sacred person, followed by the Duke's offer of a general pardon, restores the loyalty of all but a dozen of the worst rebels who are doubtful whether their offences can be covered.

In Book III Dorus informs Cleophila that Pamela, understanding that his pretended suit to Mopsa is really meant for her, has agreed to let him steal her away to the nearest sea-port, and thence to the Duchy of Thessalia. But an obstacle is the parting with his cousin, 'to whom Nature began my friendship, education confirmed it, and virtue hath made it eternal'. If therefore Cleophila will bid him stay with him, he will obey his command. But Cleophila after an inward struggle answers, 'I joy in your presence, but I joy more in your good.' It is one of the culminating points in the affectionate relationship between man and man which is one of the most attractive features of Elizabethan romance and drama.

In the further development of the Dorus and Pamela

episode Sidney displays fresh aspects of his narrative and humorous powers. In order to carry off Pamela secretly, Dorus has to get Dametas, Miso and Mopsa out of the way. In each case he accomplishes this by means of a trick. Dametas is sent off on a fool's errand to dig for buried treasure under an oak tree. Meanwhile Dorus sought out Miso 'whom he found sitting in the chimney's end, babbling to herself and showing in all her gestures that she was loathsomely weary of the world . . . having long since hated each thing else [she] was begun now to hate her self'. He entertains her with a tale of how on a hill overlooking the city of Mantinea he had seen and heard a beautiful maiden singing the loveliest of the songs in the *Arcadia*, beginning

My true love hath my heart, and I have his,
By fair exchange one for the other given,

to which a shepherd lying beside her replies with a rival poesy. And he was no other than Dametas who, after much amorous interchange, made an assignation with her about ten o'clock in a certain street in Mantinea, whither Miso rode post-haste to intercept them.

Another far-fetched tale was used by Dorus to get Mopsa out of the way. He told her how Apollo, having been cast out of heaven by Jupiter, and having served as herdsman to Admetus, had been pardoned and restored to his divinity while resting in an ash-tree near their lodge. Apollo in gratitude endowed this tree with the quality that when suitable persons sat down in it they should obtain whatsoever they wished. They must be muffled with a scarlet cloak like one that Admetus had given to Apollo, and he could lend one of his own to Mopsa. She at once seized on the opportunity and he left her in the tree, 'resolved in her heart to be the greatest lady in the world, and never after to feed on worse than frumenty.[1]

With the trio of guardians now out of the way Dorus mounted Pamela upon a horse that he had provided for her, and set out through the wildest part of the desert where he felt assured that he would meet no one till they reached a seaport where he had a bark ready for them to enter by

[1] Wheat boiled in milk.

night. But when Pamela wearied with the journey fell asleep, Dorus was so inflamed by the sight of her various beauties that he was on the point of breaking his vow to safeguard her until marriage, when there came on the scene a dozen clownish villains, armed with various kinds of weapons, whose cries wakened the sleeping princess. They were the more desperate members of the previous body of rebels who thought that their crimes would not be covered by the Duke's pardon. They overpower Dorus and Pamela and after heated discussions determine to bring the pair back to the lodge, in expectation of receiving reward from Basilius. But they are met by a band of loyal horsemen who put them to summary execution, and take charge of their prisoners.

Meanwhile Cleophila was employing various stratagems to escape the embarrassing attentions of Basilius and Gynecia. The latter was the more persistent and formidable wooer. Cleophila was forced to let her know his true sex and his status as a prince, and to pretend that she had supplanted her daughter Philoclea in his affections, to the latter's deep distress. To work out an escape from these entanglements Cleophila asks leave to retire for a time to a neighbouring cave. Here he makes an assignation for the same night with both Basilius and Gynecia who are thus without knowing it lured into each other's arms. If this is taken seriously, here at least Milton's condemnation of the *Arcadia* as a vain and amatorious poem must be allowed to stand. But do we not see some of the details of the *fabliau* peeping between the corners of the Arcadian romance, as in the description of Basilius stumbling in the darkness of the cave? 'Each coffer or cupboard he met, one saluted his shins, another his elbows, sometimes ready in revenge to strike them again with his face.' In this way Basilius fulfils part of the oracle that he would commit adultery with his own wife, which he sought to baffle.

Thus the way is left open for the fulfilment of another part of the prophecy, that his younger daughter would embrace an 'uncouth love', for Pyrocles, disguised as Cleophila, can now make his way to the lodge, where Philoclea is left unguarded. And Sidney replaces the bantering tone of the cave episodes with a subtle emotional analysis. Pyrocles on

his way to his inamorata finds that 'extremity of joy is not
without a certain joyful pain by extending the heart beyond
his wonted limits, and so forcibly holding all the fancies to
one object that it confounds their natural working'. If such
is the exquisite pain that lurks in the inmost heart of love,
has its exquisite witchery ever found more perfect interpretation in prose than in the passage that follows when
Pyrocles listens outside Philoclea's door to her singing to
her lute?

> The force of love to those poor folk that feel it is many
> ways very strange, but no way stranger than that it doth
> so enchant the lover's judgment upon her that holds the
> reins of his mind that whatsoever she doth, it ever in his
> eyes is best . . . If she sit still, that is best, for so is the
> conspiracy of her several graces held best together to make
> one perfect figure of beauty; if she walk, no doubt that is
> best, for besides the making happy the more places by
> her steps, the very stirring adds a pleasant life to her
> natural perfections. If she be silent, that without com-
> parison is best . . . But if she speak, he will take it upon
> his death, that is best.

For a time, however, the hopes of bliss entertained by
Pyrocles are dashed. His apparent preference of Gynecia has
embittered Philoclea, and he has to listen to her reproaches
until all is made clear and the lovers find rapture in each
other's arms. Love burning with so intense and pure a flame
is apparently in Sidney's eyes its own justification for complete union – at any rate in Arcadia. There is no lingering
over details, no realistic emphasis, but there is no apology,
no extenuation. It is for us to accept it as it was offered,
a fragrant Renaissance idyll, in Philoclea's own words, 'a
virtuous marriage whereto our innocent eyes were the
solemnities, and the gods themselves, the witnesses' – or once
again to turn away with Milton's condemnation on our lips.

# CHAPTER XII

# THE MANUSCRIPTS AND THE 1593 'ARCADIA' – A SUSPECTED MURDER AND POLITICAL CRISIS – EUARCHUS AS JUDGE – COUP DE THÉÂTRE

Sidney's revision of his romance was interrupted while he was engaged on Book III and henceforward the main lines of the story in the manuscripts and in the 1593 and 1598 folio versions run parallel. With Book IV Sidney, as if to display his versatile powers, returned to the comedy of Dametas and his family. The head shepherd finding after his labours no gold but a mocking couplet goes back to his lodge which he finds deserted, and where it is a relief to espy Mopsa in the ash tree. In fear of being hanged for letting Pamela escape he implores his daughter to help him, but she thinks that he is Apollo, who has taken the form and voice of Dametas, and who promises that she shall have kings as her husbands. Thus they talk at cross-purposes till Dametas is convinced that she is mad, and takes her in his arms in the hope of curing her. But his wife, returning from her fruitless journey to Mantinea, thinks that he is embracing the imaginary Charita and salutes him with a series of blows from a cudgel. When Mopsa joins in the fray Dametas steals off to the other lodge thinking that Pamela may have taken refuge there. Instead he finds Philoclea sleeping with Cleophila, whose true sex he now recognizes and proclaims to a group of shepherds, to the dishonour of the Duke. But they parry this with more tragic news – that the Duke is dead.

From this point the pastoral and humorous features of the romance are supplanted by those of a more melodramatic type. Basilius leaving the cave at dawn had discovered the deceit practised on him. In his agitation he had drained down from a gold cup a love-potion which Gynecia had brought to give to Cleophila and which had a swift and unforeseen operation. His limbs became stiff and his eyes fixed, and he

71

had time only to declare 'O, Gynecia, I die, have care.' Moved to sudden repentance the Duchess resolves to seek death by declaring herself to be the murderer of her husband. She begged the shepherds to do justice to the world, duty to their good Duke, honour to themselves, and favour to her. But they thought it a sacrilege to touch her person. Other of the shepherds gave way to lamentations for the Duke and his many excellent qualities; they ran about his body tearing their beards and garments. And to give suitable expression to their public loss they requested one of their number famed for his skill as a poet to compose an epitaph which he did in unrhymed metre.

Hereupon Philanax, the deputy ruler, having heard of the previous insurrection, arrives to place garrisons to safeguard the Duke, and to him in turn Gynecia confesses that she has murdered him. Feeling that it is his duty to take vengeance for his death Philanax places her in custody. The arrests follow of Dametas and his family, of Pyrocles whose sex has been revealed, and Musidorus, whom the loyalist horsemen had handed over to him. They are all suspected by Philanax of complicity in the death of Basilius, and this stern upholder of legality even places the two princesses in ward.

For a time the *Arcadia* turns from a romance into a political treatise on that perennial Elizabethan bogy, the difficulties and dangers of a disputed succession to the throne.

For now their Prince and guide had left them, they had not experience to rule, and had not whom to obey. Public matters had ever been privately governed, so that they had no lively taste what was good for themselves, but everything was either vehemently desirefull, or extremely terrible. . . . Altogether like a falling steeple, the parts whereof, as windows, stones and pinnacles were well, but the whole mass ruinous. And this was the general case of all, wherein notwithstanding was an extreme medley of diverse thoughts. The great men looking to make themselves strong by factions, the gentlemen some bending to them, some standing upon themselves, some to overthrow those few which were over them. The soldiers desirous of troubles as the nurse of spoil, and not much unlike to them (though in another way) were all the needy sort. The rich fearful, the wise careful.

Some were in favour of a change in the Arcadian constitution, to abolish the monarchy, and to adopt either the oligarchic Spartan, or the democratic Athenian, system. A more conservative element wished to make Philanax ruler in place of Basilius, but he had his enemies, especially the ambitious and unscrupulous Tymantus who counted virtue only a 'School name'. He incited the Arcadian nobles against Philanax as a hypocrite and self-seeker. 'Let us,' he cried, 'deliver the Duchess and our natural Princesses and leave them no longer under his authority, whose proceedings would rather show that he has himself been the murderer of the Duke than a fit guardian for his posterity.' But another unexpected complication follows. Kerxenes, the Marrtinean, who had been the host of the two Princes on their first arrival in Arcadia, though he did not know their princely status, had been so impressed by their nobility of bearing that he advocated that they should be jointly raised to the vacant throne.

Such was the critical situation at the close of Book IV. With the opening of Book V help came suddenly from a friendly foreign source. Euarchus, King of Macedon, father and uncle of the two Princes, had been perturbed by the news of the temporary abdication of Basilius, who had long been his faithful ally. He was afraid that, with Arcadia leaderless, an attack might be made on the Greek confederacy by the Asiatics on the one side or the Latins on the other. He had therefore set sail and arrived in Arcadia with a company of only twenty men in the hope of persuading Basilius to resume his active duties, only in time to hear of his sudden death. The news of his arrival was brought to Philanax, who saw in it a providential dispensation for restoring unity among the Arcadians. He appealed to them to put the ordering of all things into the hands of Euarchus, and setting out to meet him he begged him to become the 'elected Protector of the Dukedom'. Euarchus, taken aback by this startling proposal, hesitated for a time, declaring, 'I must be fully informed how the patient is minded before I can promise to undertake the cure.' But in the end yielding to the arguments of Philanax he agreed to take upon himself the judgment of the present case. Together they rode to the lodges where they were received by the crowd with acclamation. Euarchus warned them not to expect too much of him, as he was a fallible creature, and issued his first order that no one under heavy penalty should call him by any other name than Protector of Arcadia, 'for I will not leave any possible colour to any of my natural successors to make claim to this which by free election you have bestowed upon me, and so I vow unto you to depose myself of it, as soon as the judgement is passed, the Duke buried, and his lawful successor appointed'. In accordance with Arcadian custom he ordered that the trial of the accused should take place as speedily as possible on the following day.

Then in another display of his versatile skill Sidney depicts the states of mind of the various prisoners waiting their doom. First there is the appalling picture of Gynecia in almost total darkness blaspheming and imagining 'she saw strange sights and that she heard the cry of hellish ghosts'. Sorrowful too was the state of Pamela and Philoclea, but as 'they had not consented to so much evil . . . so were at greater peace with themselves'. And as they were together they could confide to each other the story of their loves, followed by crying and wringing of hands, by wishes and finally prayers. Meanwhile Pyrocles and Musidorus, under the strongest guard, were concerned only with the safety of their two ladies, and with either of them taking the responsibility for the misfortunes that had befallen them. But these weigh for nothing in the balance against the love of 'these matchless creatures'. In the debate that follows which falls, as it were, into dialogue form, is it fanciful to hear echoes of the disputations in Sidney's Oxford days?

> *Pyrocles:* I call all the gods to witness . . . no shame, no torment, nor death could make me forego the least part of the inward honour, essential pleasure and living life I have enjoyed in the presence of the faultless Philoclea.
>
> *Musidorus:* Take the pre-eminence in all things but in true

loving, for the confession of that no death shall get out of me.

*Pyr:* (soberly smiling) I perceive we shall have a debate in the other world, if at least there remain any thing of remembrance in that place.

*Mus:* I do not think the contrary, although you know it is greatly held that with the death of body and senses (which are not only the beginning but dwelling and nourishing of passions, thoughts and imaginations) they failing, memory likewise fails, which riseth only out of them, and thus is there left nothing but the intellectual part or intelligence . . . utterly void from the possibility of drawing to itself these sensible considerations.

*Pyr:* Certainly, I easily yield that we shall not know one another, and much less those past things with a sensible or passionate knowledge, for the cause being taken away the effect follows. Neither do I think we shall have such a memory as now we have, which is but a relic of the senses, or rather a print the senses have left of things past in our thoughts. But it shall be a vital power of that very intelligence which, as while it was here, it held the chief seat of our life, and was, as it were, the last resort to which of all our knowledges the highest appeal came, and so by that means was never ignorant of our actions (though many times rebelliously resisted, always with this prison darkened): So much more being free of this prison, and returning to the life of all things where all infinite knowledge is, it cannot but be a right intelligence which is both his name and being of things both present and past. . . . At that second delivery of us, void of sensible memory or memorative passin, we shall not see the colours but lives of all things that have been or can be. And shall (as I hope) know our friendship, though exempt from the earthly care of friendship, having both united it and ourselves in that high and heavenly love of the unquenchable Light.

In this speech of Pyrocles the old *Arcadia* reaches its loftiest height, and it is no wonder that Musidorus, 'with a heavenly joy upon him', responds to it with a song of his own composing, making light of the fear of death.

By the next day the procedure for the judgment was completed. Euarchus, clothed in black, took his seat on the Throne of Judgment which had been occupied by Basilius for the trial of criminals. In front of him was the body of the Duke covered with a mantle. Round about stood the populace, commanded to keep silence. On their way to trial Musidorus made an eloquent plea for Pamela, and Pyrocles for Philoclea, which were sympathetically received by the crowd. Then Philanax began an indictment of Gynecia, which she at once interrupted.

I have been too cruel an executioner over mine own soul to desire that execution of justice should be stayed for me . . . I therefore say to thee (O just Judge) that I and only I was the worker of Basilius' death; they were these hands that gave unto him that poisonous potion that hath brought death unto him and loss to Arcadia. It was I, and none but I that hastened his aged years to an unnatural end, and have made all this people orphans of their royal father. I am the subject that have killed my Prince; I am the wife that have murdered my husband; I was a degenerate woman, an undoer of this country, a shame of my children. What more couldest thou have said, O Philanax? And all this I grant.

She begged therefore for a speedy death, and by her words and bearing moved the multitude to compassion. But Euarchus after consultation with the chief Arcadians felt that in both private and public respects she had heinously offended. His sentence therefore was that she be kept a close prisoner till the day of her husband's burial, when she was to be interred living beside his body.

The two Princes were the next defendants, and gave their names as Tymophirus, Despota of Licia and Palladius, Prince of Caria, under which Euarchus did not recognize their relationship to him. Philanax in the role of prosecutor

entered upon a passionate and prolonged indictment of
Pyrocles, who with some impatience endured the length of
his oration. When it ended with hypocritical sighs and tears
Pyrocles declared that his answer would be simple and naked
truth, and he related how love of the two Princesses had
inspired all their actions since they had landed in Arcadia.
Let the case be decided by friendly combat, in which Philanax would be armed, while he stood merely in his shirt.
Euarchus, however, refused to let the verdict depend upon
force and ordered that proceedings should be taken against
Musidorus.

Meanwhile Philanax had suppressed evidence in favour
of the two prisoners. These were letters in their favour by
Philoclea on behalf of Pyrocles and by Pamela on behalf of
Musidorus, which a henchman of Philanax brought to him
and which he left unread. Philanax, in addition to the crime
against Basilius, made the chief charge against Musidorus
that he had tried to take out of Arcadia Pamela, who after
her father's death was its lawful ruler, and that this was an
act of treason. Musidorus retorted that Pyrocles and himself
had saved the life of the Duke during the rebellion, and that
Pamela had sought to escape from her conditions in Dametas'
household of her own free will. After weighing the arguments on both sides, Euarchus pronounced that according
to the Arcadian laws Tymophirus (Pyrocles) should be
thrown to death from a high tower, and Palladius (Musidorus) should be beheaded by Dametas who was to remain
a life-long executioner.

But before the sentences could be carried out there arrived
from Thessalia a retainer of Musidorus named Kalodulus to
whom Menalcas had brought earlier tidings of his Prince.
Seeking to inform Euarchus of these he had followed him
to Arcadia and had been informed of the recent proceedings.
Falling at the feet of Euarchus he had told him that 'Those
he had judged were his own son and nephew, the one the
comfort of Macedon, the other the stay of Thessalia.' But
to the amazement of all present Euarchus refused to alter his
sentences. 'No, no, Pyrocles and Musidorus, I prefer you
much before mine own life, but I prefer justice as far before
you . . . For my part I must tell you, you have forced a father

to rob himself of his children.' None the less Pyrocles made one last appeal not for himself but for Musidorus.

O father, vouchsafe, I say, to let the few and last words your son shall ever speak not be tedious unto you. . . . O save the life of this Prince; that is the only all I will with my last breath demands of you . . . Let Musidorus live, and Pyrocles shall live in him, and you will not want a child.

As Pyrocles ended his speech those near the Duke's body heard 'a great voice of groaning from under the velvet covering', and it was found that the Duke still lived. The drink taken by Basilius was neither a love-potion nor a deadly poison, but a draught that brought on a sleep of thirty hours which had all the appearance of death. Such it had been assumed to be by all, though nowhere had this been explicitly stated. And Sidney prolonged the tension of the trial scenes because he knew that by this *coup-de-théâtre* he would give relief to the agonized emotions of his readers. Basilius now understands the Delphic Oracle's prophecy, 'in thy throne a foreign State shall sit'. All ends happily, with reconciliation between him and Gynecia, marriage bells for the lovers, and rewards for those who have played loyal parts.

# CHAPTER XIII

# THE NEW 'ARCADIA' – KALANDER'S HOUSE - ARGALUS AND PARTHENIA

An attempt to make a general comparison between this old *Arcadia* and the uncompleted revised form is deferred to after a summary of the latter. It appeared in two editions. The first of these, published in quarto by Ponsonby, was dated 1590, and was prefaced by Philip's letter to his sister and by the following note:

> The division and summing of the chapters was not of Sir Philip Sidney's doing, but architectured by the over-seer of the print, for the more ease of the readers. He therefore submits himself to their judgment, and, if his labour answers not the worthiness of the book, desireth pardon for it. As also if any defect be found in the Eclogues, which although they were of Sir Philip Sidney's writing, yet even they not perused by him, but left till the work had been finished, that then choice should have been made, which should have been taken, and in what manner brought in. At this time they have been chosen and disposed as the over-seer thought best.

The 'over-seer' was in all probability Greville, and the version for which he was responsible ended abruptly in the middle of Chapter 29 of the third Book. The Countess of Pembroke was evidently dissatisfied with this, for in 1593 Ponsonby issued a folio edition, 'Now since the first edition augmented and ended.' A preface to the 'gentle reader' by H. S. (the Earl of Pembroke's secretary, Henry Sandford) declared: 'The disfigured face wherewith this work not long since appeared in the common view moved that noble Lady to whose honour it was consecrated, to whose protection it was committed, to take in hand the wiping away those spots wherewith the beauties thereof were unworthily blemished.' This abusive language was too strong, though the emendations in the 1593 text, where it ran parallel to that of 1590, were numerous.[1] H.S. had more justification for the further claim: 'But often as in repairing a ruinous house, the mending of some old part occasioned the making of some new: so here her honourable labour begun in correcting the faults, ended in supplying the defects.' The Countess had supplemented the narrative where it had been broken off in the revised version of 1590 by the addition of the latter part of Book III and Books IV and V.[2] But she or Sandford had done a disservice to readers of the romance by omitting the chapter divisions with headlines which acted as clues through the complicated narrative. Nor were these restored in the 1598 folio which included the *Arcadia* with Sidney's other chief works.

Whatever his motives may have been, Sidney in his revised version completely transformed the beginning of his romance. In deference apparently to the fashionable convention he first introduces two shepherds, Claius and Strephon, lamenting the departure of the beautiful Urania: 'Hath not the only love of her made us being silly, ignorant shepherds, raise up our thoughts above the ordinary level of the world so as great clerks do not disdain our conference? Hath not the desire to seem worthy in her eyes made us, when others were sleeping, to sit viewing the course of the heavens? When others were running at base, to run over learned writings?'

This lament is suddenly cut short by the sight of a young man's body being washed up from the sea, which, after compassionate treatment by them, gives signs of life; 'crying upon the name of Pyrocles . . . and shall Musidorus live after Pyrocles?', whereupon he attempted to cast himself back into the sea, but the shepherds prevented him. They then engaged some fishermen to put to sea to search for Pyrocles whom they saw floating, clinging to a mast and whom they might have rescued but for the arrival on the scene of a pirate ship from which they fled in terror, while it picked up Pyrocles.

Thus Sidney interests his readers in the fortunes of the

---

[1] See Zandvoort, op. cit., p. 23.
[2] There were, however, a number of changes in detail, analysed y Zandvoort, op. cit.. pp. 26–40.

royal cousins before he tells of Basilius and his family, or even sets foot in Arcadia itself. For the shepherds let him know that they are in Laconia, where they are strangers, but that they will guide him to the neighbouring country of Arcadia, where dwells a gentleman called Kalander,[1] renowned for his hospitality, in whose house he will recover his health. On the third morning after journeying through the bleak countryside of Laconia, Musidorus was delighted with the prospect or Arcadia.

There were hills which garnished their proud heights with stately trees; humble valleys whose bare estate seemed comforted with the refreshing of silver rivers; meadows enameled with all sorts of eye-pleasing flowers; thickets, which being lined with most pleasant shade, were witnessed so to by the cheerful deposition of many well-tuned birds; each pasture stored with sheep feeding with sober security, while the pretty lambs with bleating oratory craved the dams' comfort; here a shepherd's boy piping, as though he should never be old; there a young shepherdess knitting and withal singing, and it seemed that her voice comforted her hands to work, and her hands kept time to her voice's music.

This is one of the descriptive set pieces characteristic of Sidney's later style, closing in a chain figure.

Kalander not only saw Musidorus (who called himself Palladius) through six weeks of burning fever, but sent out a ship and a galley in search of Pyrocles under the name of Daiphantus. When his guest had recovered, Kalander showed him the beauties of his house, especially 'a well arrayed ground' behind it, which was neither field, garden, nor orchard, or rather it was both field, garden, and orchard. And Sidney displays the enthusiasm of a landscape-gardener in describing the fair pond in the middle of the place, and the fountain, 'a naked Venus of white marble' with the infant Æneas at her breast, and a summer-house full of delightful pictures. Most of these were of classical beauties, but one large painting contained a comely old man with a

[1]Kerxenus in the old *Arcadia*.

lady of middle age, but of excellent beauty, and between them a young maid, who outrivals her. On Palladius inquiring who she was Kalander answered that she was Philoclea, the younger daughter of their Prince, and thence was led on to tell his guest the strange story of Basilius's visit to the Oracle, his temporary abdication in favour of Philanax and his measures to safeguard his two daughters. In Kalander's differentiation between them Sidney again introduces a notable set piece.

The elder is called Pamela, by many men not deemed inferior to her sister: for my part when I marked them both, me thought there was (if at least such perfections may receive the word of more) more sweetness to Philoclea but more majesty in Pamela; me thought love played in Philoclea's eyes, and threatened in Pamela's: me thought Philoclea's beauty only persuaded, but so persuaded as all must yield; Pamela's beauty used violence, and such violence as no heart could resist. And it seems that such proportion is between their minds, Philoclea so bashful as though her excellencies had stolen into her before she was aware; so humble that she will put all pride out of countenance: in sum, such proceeding as will stir hope, but teach hope good manners. Pamela of high thoughts, who avoids not pride with not knowing her excellencies, but by making that one of her excellencies to be void of pride; her mother's wisdom, greatness, nobility, but (if I can guess aright) knit with a more constant temper.

In the original *Arcadia* Philoclea's portrait had at once inspired Pyrocles with love, but the revised version meanwhile calls attention to other happenings. News comes to Kalander of the capture of his son Clitophon by the Helots in a battle against the gentlemen of Lacedemon, and the steward informs Musidorus of how this has come about. When Basilius married Gynecia she was accompanied by a young kinsman Argalus, who made his home in Arcadia and won the devoted friendship of Clitophon, who brought him to the house of his aunt, where he won the love of her daughter, Parthenia. But she had been courted, with her mother's approval, by a rich noble of Laconia; Demagoras, and the day of their 'assurance', was near.

Yet love, that saw he had a great journey to make in short time, hasted so himself that before the word could tie her to Demagoras, her heart hath vowed her to Argalus, with so grateful a receipt in mutual affection that if she desired above all things to have Argalus, Argalus feared nothing but to miss Parthenia.

She told her mother she would first be bedded in her grave than wedded to Demagoras. When that domineering lady died, Demagoras, thinking that Parthenia was now her own mistress, took the ghastly revenge of seizing her and rubbing her face with a most horrible poison which made her loathsome to look upon. For this he was banished on pain of death but joined himself with all his resources to the rebel Helots.

In spite of this outrage Argalus remained faithful to his love for Parthenia, but she would give no ear to his entreaties, and had finally stolen away by night, and it was unknown what had become of her. After long and fruitless search Argalus, in order to be revenged on Demagoras, made his way to the Helots' headquarters and inflicted on his rival a mortal wound, but was himself taken prisoner, and was expecting execution. To seek to rescue him Clitophon, with some Laconian noblemen and forces gathered by them, attacked a young man whom Demagoras had appointed his successor, but was defeated and taken prisoner, though he was less closely confined than Argalus.

'Thus,' ends the steward, 'I have delivered all I understand touching the loss of my Lord's son, and the cause thereof, which though it was not necessary for Clitophon's case to be so particularly told: yet the strangeness of it made me think it would not be unpleasant unto you.' Is Sidney here excusing himself for what was a new departure in the revised *Arcadia*, the introduction in the story of Argalus and Parthenia of what may be called a novelette, independent of the main romance? It so worked upon Palladius that he devised a stratagem by which he deceived the Helots into letting him at the head of a considerable force enter the town where the prisoners were held. But before they could be set free, the Helots were rallied by their new young captain who engaged in a duel with Palladius, whom he struck upon the side of his head, so that his helmet fell off. And then another strange thing happened.

His chief enemy, instead of pursuing that advantage, kneeled down, offering to deliver the pommel of his sword in token of yielding; withal speaking aloud unto him that he thought it more liberty to be his prisoner than any other's general. Palladius standing upon himself, and misdoubting some craft, and the Helots that were next their captain wavering between looking for some stratagem or fearing treason; 'What,' said the captain, 'hath Palladius forgotten the voice of Daiphantus?' By that watchword Palladius knew that it was his only friend Pyrocles, whom he had lost upon the sea, and therefore both most full of wonder so to be met . . . caused the retreat to be sounded . . . But indeed the chief parter of the fray was the night, which with her black arms pulled their malicious sights one from the other.

After a parley between both sides an agreement was made, chiefly through the influence of Daiphantus, by which on the withdrawal of the invading Arcadians, Palladius, with Clitophon and his father, was set at liberty while Daiphantus promised soon to join them and bring Argalus, if pardoned, with him. In a few days he arrived with Argalus at Kalander's house. 'All that beheld him (and all that might behold him did behold him) made their eyes quick messengers to their minds that there there they had seen the uttermost that in mankind might be seen.' Soon Fortune had a surprise for Kalander's guests. A young noble lady was announced, whom Kalander at once took to be his niece Parthenia, owing to the likeness between them. But she asked to be allowed to speak with Argalus, and told him that Parthenia had come to the court of Queen Helen of Corinth. 'I took the best care I could of her, and of her understood the whole tragical history of her undeserved adventure, and therewithal of that most noble constancy in you, my Lord Argalus.' Before her death a few days ago Parthenia had persuaded her to think of no husband but Argalus, 'as of the only man in the world worthy to be loved', and she had now come to offer herself to him. Argalus, after declaring that he was infinitely bound to her, and that she had made him her slave, continued:

> Excellent lady, know that if my heart were mine to give, you before all other should have it, but Parthenia's it is, though dead; there I began, there I end, all matter of affection. I hope I shall not long tarry after her, with whose beauty if I had only been in love, I should be so with you who have the same beauty. But it was Parthenia's self I loved, and love, which no likeness can make one, no commandment dissolve, no faults defile, nor no death finish.

To her protest against the disgrace of being refused he answered, 'it is only happiness I refuse, since of the only happiness I could and can desire I am refused'. Thereupon she ran to him and embracing him cried, 'Why, then, Argalus, take thy Parthenia.' It was indeed she who had been cured by a pre-eminent physician at Queen Helen's court, and who was soon afterwards wedded to Argalus. Sidney ends this tale of a truly spiritual love with an appropriate image. 'As she went to the temple to be married, her eyes themselves seemed a temple, wherein love and beauty were married.'

Meanwhile Diaphantus had entertained Palladius with a recital of his adventures since he and his cousin had been separated in the sea after leaping overboard from the burning ship. The pirate ship which had picked him up was attacked by some royal Laconian galleys, and the pirates in their own defence set their prisoners free. It chanced that in the contest Daiphantus killed Euryleon, the King's nephew, but the royal forces were victorious, and he was strictly jailed in the town of Temaria. But the populace conspired with the Helots, broke open the jails, and set him free. In gratitude he performed such feats on their behalf in some conflicts that followed that they elected him their captain in successor to Demagoras. And after peace had been made, he was ready to seek Palladius throughout the world but now happily they were met.

To entertain his guests Kalander organized a hunting party, in the account of which Sidney shows his interest in the sport. At its close Daiphantus, who had lately shown a desire to be alone, was not to be found, but he had left a letter for Palladius telling him that 'violence of love leads me into such a course, whereof your knowledge may much more vex you than help me. Therefore pardon my concealing it from you, since, if I wrong you, it is in the respect I bear you.' Palladius had to read the letter twice or thrice before taking in its meaning, and then exclaimed:

Ah, Pyrocles, what means this alteration? What have I deserved of thee to be thus banished of thy counsels? Heretofore I have accused the sea; condemned the pirates, and hated my evil fortune that deprived me of thee. But now thyself is the sea, which drowns my comfort, thyself is the pirate that robs thyself of me; thy own will becomes my evil fortune.

He thereupon told Kalander that Daiphantus had been recalled to Laconia to take measures on behalf of his dependants there, and that it was fitting that he should follow him privately. He arrayed himself in a suit of black armour, 'as either a badge or a prognostication of his mind', and took his leave, accompanied only by Clitophon, who had entreated to rejoin his lord Daiphantus. This serves to introduce the second novelette of *Amphialus and Queen Helen*.

# CHAPTER XIV

# 'AMPHIALUS AND QUEEN HELEN' – THE CHALLENGE OF PHALANTUS

After a fruitless search in many towns Palladius and Clitophon rode to a pleasant valley where the latter espied a piece of armour and subsequently other pieces, together with a head-piece and shield which Clitophon recognized as belonging to his cousin, Amphialus; 'whom the fame of the world seemed to set in balance with any Knight living'. Palladius put on the armour whereby he thought he might get news of Amphialus, and travelling a little further 'they met with a coach drawn with four milk-white horses furnished all in black, with a black-a-moor boy upon every horse, they all apparelled in white, the coach itself very richly furnished in black and white'. Before they could see who was inside they were set upon by over a dozen horsemen who bade them yield themselves prisoners or die. But Palladius, backed by Clitophon, left their attackers lifeless or sorely wounded, and then looking into the coach saw at one end a lady of great beauty, darkened by sorrow; at the other two attendant women, 'holding before them a picture, in which was a goodly gentleman painted, having in their faces a certain waiting sorrow'. The lady recognizing the armour took Palladius to be Amphialus and reproached him, 'You have enough punishment; it is time for cruelty to leave you and evil fortune me.' Palladius told her her mistake, and how he had found the armour, whereupon she begged him to escort her to the nearest town, while he in return asked for a recital of her fortunes, which were as follows:

She was by birth Helen, Queen of Corinth, accepted by the people after her father's death, and loved by them. Her Court soon swarmed with suitors for her hand, among whom was Philoxenus, son and heir to the noble Timotheus, whom she less misliked than any of the rest, which in some proportion her countenance delivered unto him. 'Though I must protest it was a very false ambassador if it delivered at all

any affection, whereof her heart was utterly void.' One day
Philoxenus brought with him a friend, Amphialus, on whose
picture she was now gazing, and on whom she lavished
praise and endearments. He was the nephew of Basilius, the
King[1] of Arcadia, and had been his heir till by his marriage
late in life he had begotten his two daughters. He had been
sent to be a companion to Philoxenus in the house of Timotheus, who loved him no less than his own son. Every trial
of Amphialus proved to be a step to greater fame, and closer
friendship with Philoxenus, who finally made use of it by
bringing him to Queen Helen's Court to further his suit.
But 'while he pleaded for another, he won me for himself, if
at least (with that she sighed) he would account it a winning,
for his fame had so framed the way to my mind that his
presence so full of beauty, sweetness, and noble conversation
had entered there before he vouchsafed to call for the keys.
O Lord, how did my soul hang on his lips while he spoke.'
At last she had revealed her feeling to him, only to 'receive
a most resolute refusal of himself', followed by his departure
on distant travel. When Philoxenus had again sought her
favour, she told him that she would hear him more willingly
if he would speak for Amphialus as well as Amphialus had
done for him, to which he made no answer; but went away
pale and quaking. Overtaking Amphialus he called him
traitor and coward, and struck him mighty blows with his
sword. Amphialus at first refused to fight, but at last re-
taliating in self-defence by mischance gave Philoxenus a
mortal wound. Nor was this the end. The aged Timotheus,
coming in quest of his son, and finding him lifeless, was so
overcome that he sank to the earth and died. Overwhelmed
by the double tragedy of father and son Amphialus threw
away his armour, which Palladius was now wearing, and ran
into the thickest of the woods, whence he sent a message to
the Queen that of all creatures in the world he hated her
most. Therefore she had left her country, risking all perils
and dishonours, only to follow him who proclaims his hate
of her. At his request Palladius entrusted her to the care
of Clitophon to take her to the next town, while he continued
his search for Daiphantus.

[1] In the old *Arcadia* he was Duke.

After two months' fruitless travel he returned to Arcadia, and then one day near the mountain Moembus he came upon a lady whose face he could not perfectly see because she walked with her side towards him, but whose head-dress and costume gave occasion for another descriptive set-piece:

Well might he perceive the hanging of her hair in fairest quality, in locks some curled and some as it were forgotten, with such a careless care, and an art so hiding art, that she seemed she would lay them for a pattern, whether nature simply, or nature helped by cunning, be more excellent; the rest whereof was drawn with a coronet of gold, richly set with pearl, and so joined all over with gold wires, and covered with feathers of divers colours that it was not unlike to a helmet, such glittering show it bore, and so bravely was it held up from the head. Upon her body she wore a doublet of sky-coloured satin, covered with plates of gold, and as it were, nailed with precious stones, that in it she might seem armed; the nether parts of her garment was so full of stuff and cut after such a fashion that though the length of it reached to the ankles, yet in her going one might sometimes discern the small of her leg which with the foot was dressed in a short pair of crimson velvet buskins, in some places open (as the ancient manner was) to show the fairness of the skin.

Over all this was a mantle, clasped by a very rich jewel, and on her thigh she wore a sword, a witness that she was an Amazon. Entering an arbour she sang a song beginning, 'Transformed in show, and more transformed in mind,' and ending,

What marvel then I take a woman's hue,
Since what I see, think, know, is all but you?

The words of the song, and still more the voice of the singer, gave Musidorus the belief that the Amazon was Pyrocles disguised, and so it proved. Thereupon followed in similar fashion as in the original version the attempt of Musidorus to persuade his cousin to renounce love and its evil effects, not to 'overthrow all the excellent things you have done which have filled the world with your fame, as if you should drown your ship in the long desired haven, or like an ill player should mar the last Act of his tragedy'. This simile is an incidental illustration of Sidney's critical interest in the stage of his day. At last, however, Musidorus had to give way to the strength of his cousin's passion, of whose origin he then gave an account. It had been inspired by the picture of Philoclea in Kalander's gallery, but the revised version, with its extended scope, indicates that this had a link with an earlier unfortunate love affair of Pyrocles, as he found Philoclea 'much resembling, though, I must say, much surpassing the lady Zelmane whom too well I loved. But this was a more wounding impression of that wonderful passion which to be defined is impossible, because no words reach to the strange nature of it: they only know it which inwardly feel it: it is called love.' And as Pyrocles enlarges on how each thing he saw figured out some parts of his passions, there is an unexpected throw-back to the first novelette, 'When even Parthenia's fair face became a lecture to me of Philoclea's imagined beauty, and of Zelmane 'for that dear lady's sake to whose memory I am so much bound'.

His encounter thus disguised with Dametas, and his first interview with Basilius and his family are described by Pyrocles in much the same terms as in the original narrative, but he rises to novel ecstasy at the sight of Philoclea.

But when the ornament of the earth, the model of heaven, the triumph of nature, the light of beauty, queen of love, young Philoclea, appeared in her nymph-like apparel, so near nakedness as one might well discern part of her perfections; and yet so apparelled as did she show she kept best store of her beauty to herself; her hair (alas, too poor a word, why should I not rather call them her beams?) drawn up into a net able to take Jupiter when he was in the form of an eagle; her body (O sweet body) covered with a light taffeta garment so cut as the wrought smock came through it in many places, enough to have made your restrained imagination have thought what was under it: with the cast of her black eyes, black indeed, whether nature so made them that we might be the more able to behold and bear their wonderful shining, or that she (goddess like) would work the miracle in herself, in giving blackness the price above all beauty.

Pyrocles, after accepting the invitation to remain with them in the lodge, realizes that Basilius has fallen in love with him as Zelmane, and the sharp-eyed Gynecia with him in his true sex. It was 'a notable dumb show of Cupid's Kingdom.'

But here again the interest of the romance is diverted from the central figures to a newcomer, Phalantus of Corinth, who challenges any Arcadian Knight that 'the defendant should bring his mistress's picture, which being set by the image of Artesia (so was the mistress of Phalantus named) who in six courses should have better of the other, in the judgement of Basilius, with him both the honour and the pictures should remain'. Artesia, though not in love with Phalantus, had adopted him as her servant, and on his saying how much he would do for her sake had charged him to go with her through all the Courts of Greece, and give her beauty the principality over all other. Phalantus, perplexed but bound by his promise, had fought successfully in many Greek Courts, and a number of defeated Knights 'had forfeited the picture of their ladies, to give a forced false testimony to Artesia's excellence'. He made his entry after Artesia seated in a triumphant chariot drawn by four winged horses. Before her marched two-in-two footmen carrying the pictures of the ladies whose champions Phalantus had defeated, of whom a colourful description is given. It is somewhat surprising to find Queen Helen, Parthenia and the shepherdess Ourania among them. Again Phalantus proves victor in a number of contests, though there was little to choose between him and Clitophon who had again taken up the gage on behalf of Queen Helen. Then followed almost at the same time two Knights, one very ill-apparelled in old-fashioned armour, the other attired all in black. After a dispute on precedence this was given to the former, who struck Phalantus, still in his saddle, from his horse, and brought his almost completed enterprise to an end in disgrace. And Sidney adds with acid humour:

Phalantus' disgrace was ingrieved in lieu of comfort by Artesia who telling him she never looked for other, bid him seek some other mistress. He, excusing himself, and turning over the fault to fortune, 'then let that be your ill fortune too', said she, 'that you have lost me'. 'Nay truly, madam,' said Phalantus, 'it shall not be so, for I think the loss of such a mistress will prove a great gain'; and so concluded, to the sport of Basilius, to see young folks' love that came in masked with so great pomp, go out with so little constancy.

Then follows one of the surprises which are characteristic of Sidney's technique. The ill-apparelled Knight pulls off his helmet, and shows himself to be Zelmane, who had stolen forth and borrowed an old suit of armour, in order to redeem Philoclea's picture from captivity. All vied in doing honour to the Amazon, whom daily they sought with some or other sports to delight.

Then follows without change in essentials from the original version the conversion of Musidorus by Pamela's beauty into a slave of love, his entrance with a feigned tale as a herdsman into the service of Dametas, and the incursion into the pastoral sports of two savage beasts, when he saves Pamela from a she-bear, and Pyrocles rescues Philoclea from a lion. And to lighten the emotional stress of these episodes Sidney draws again the picture of Dametas,

lying with his head and breast, as far as he could thrust himself into a bush, drawing up his legs as close unto him as he could. For, (like a man of a very kind nature soon to take pity of himself) he was fully resolved not to see his own death. And when Dorus pushed him, bidding him be of good cheer, it was a great while ere we could persuade him that Dorus was not the bear, so that he was fain to pull him out by the heels, and show him the beast as dead as he could wish it, which you may believe me was a very joyful sight unto him. But then he forgot all courtesy, for he fell upon the beast, giving it many a manful wound, swearing by much it was not well such beasts should be suffered in a commonwealth.

And, as if in answer, there came a message from Cecropia, the vindictive sister-in-law of Basilius, mother of Amphialus, that the beasts had escaped from one of her keepers who deserved punishment. Basilius merely replied that Cecropia should kill all such beasts in her possession. But Gynecia thought it probable that what had happened was due to some mischievous practice rather than misfortune.

Gynecia herself appears in no favourable light at the beginning of Book II, where she reveals her passion for Zelmane, and her jealousy of Philoclea, first in a soliloquy and then to the astonished Amazon. But their colloquy is interrupted by Basilius, singing,

> Let not old age disgrace my high desire,
> O heavenly maid, in human shape contained.

He bids Gynecia return to the lodge, as he has matters of State to discuss with Zelmane, but these prove to be another bewildering declaration of love, which Zelmane can greet only with silence, and then depart to consider how she can rid herself of her 'intricate troubles'. She seeks out Musidorus 'that upon the shoulders of friendship she might lay the burthen of sorrow', but finds that her cousin has his own tale of difficulties in love to tell. He has to manoeuvre to win Pamela's ear by paying pretended suit to Mopsa, and has to reveal indirectly his previous fortunes and true status. All this is disclosed by Pamela to Philoclea in a midnight colloquy when they are in bed together. And she tells, in another of Sidney's incidental theatrical references, how the supposed shepherd Dorus would appear in various inventions before her to testify his love.

> One time he danced the matachine dance[1] in armour (O, with what a graceful dexterity!) . . . another time he persuaded his master, to make my time seem shorter, in manner of a dialogue to play Priamus while he played Paris. Think, sweet Philoclea, what a Priamus we had: but truly my Paris was a Paris, and more than a Paris, who, while in a savage apparel, with naked neck, arms and legs, he made love to Oenone, you might well see by his

[1] A sword dance, in which the dancers wore fantastic costumes.

changed countenance and the tears that he felt the part he played.

When at last Philoclea saw that Pamela was sleeping, she murmured, 'Alas she weeps because she would be no sooner happy: I weep because I can never be happy; her tears flow from pity, mine from being too far lower than the reach of pity.'

# CHAPTER XV

# RECITALS BY MUSIDORUS AND PAMELA

Next morning Pamela, in order to keep Musidorus in talk with her, questioned him about his friend Pyrocles, supposed to have been drowned, and his father, Euarchus, King of Macedonia. In the description of the latter Sidney pictures his ideal sovereign.

He, when he came to the crown, finding by his late ancestors' either negligence or misfortune, that in some ages many of those duties [homage by minor Greek kings] had been intermitted, would never stir up old titles, how apparent soever, whereby the public peace (with the loss of many not guilty souls) should be broken . . . Who, as he was most wise to see what was best, and most just in the performing what he saw, and temperate in abstaining from anything any way contrary: so . . . no thought can imagine a greater heart to see and condemn danger, where danger would offer to make any wrongful threatening upon him. A Prince that indeed especially measured his greatness by his goodness; and, if for anything he loved greatness, it was because therein he might exercise his goodness.

With such a beneficent polity Sidney, though the mouth of Musidorus, contrasts the evils of oligarchical rule, where a few great lords, 'having the power of Kings but not the nature of Kings', exercise unjust authority, showing favoratism and stamping out liberty.

From this excursus on the art of government Musidorus proceeds further with his story. Dorilaus, Prince of Thessalia, married the sister of Euarchus, and he was their son. Euarchus in turn married the sister of Dorilaus, and they had a child, Pyrocles, four years younger[1] than his cousin. Owing to the deaths of Dorilaus and the mother of Pyrocles, King Euarchus sent his child to the care of his sister to be

[1] In the earlier version he was only one year younger.

95

brought up with his cousin. The growth of the pair in affectionate friendship was already familiar, but for the first time
it is now told how they came to be together on the wrecked
ship near the coast of Laconia. At a crisis in a war which
Euarchus was waging against allied enemies the cousins
fitted out a flotilla to go to his help. We do not generally
think of Sidney in the role of an Elizabethan seaman, but he
here gives, as if from personal experience, two vividly contrasted pictures of ships in a calm, and a storm-tossed, sea.
At first all went well.

> The wind was like a servant, waiting behind them so just
> that they might fill the sails as they listed . . . they all kept
> together like a beautiful flock which so well could obey
> their master's pipe; without sometimes, to delight the
> Princes' eyes, some two or three of them would strive
> who could (either by the cunning of spending the wind's
> breath, or by the advantageous building of their moving
> houses) leave their fellows behind them in the honour of
> speed . . . And so the Princes . . . seeing wherein the sea-
> discipline differed from land service, they had for a day
> and almost a whole night as pleasing entertainment as the
> falsest heart could give to him he meant worst to.

This deceitful calm suddenly gave way to black fog, with
storm, hail and rain.

> Then the tumultuous sea began to swell in pride against
> the afflicted navy . . . making mountains of itself, over
> which the tossed and tottering ships should climb, to be
> straight carried down to a pit of hellish darkness, with
> such cruel blows against the sides of the ship (that which
> way soever it went was still in his malice) that there was
> left neither power to stay, nor way to escape. And shortly
> had it so dissevered the loving company, which the day
> before had tarried together, that most of them never met
> again, but were swallowed up in his never satisfied mouth.

Among the survivors were the two Princes who owed their
lives to the self-sacrifice of two dependants, whom they had
redeemed from captivity, and who now chose to risk death

in the waves rather than overload the rib of the vessel which could only support two.

Then follows from the lips of Musidorus an account of the subsequent adventures of Pyrocles and himself which delayed their arrival in Arcadia. Pyrocles, beaten and bruised by the tempestuous sea, landed in Phrygia, whose King was a tyrant of a melancholy nature, 'suspecting, or rather condemning, all men of evil because his mind had no eye to espy goodness'. He determined to put Pyrocles to death and appointed a day for his execution. But news of this reached Musidorus, who had been rescued by a fisherman of the Kingdom of Pontus, and who now offered himself as a victim instead of Pyrocles. The Phrygian King, frightened by a prophecy about Musidorus which boded ill to himself, eagerly accepted this more welcome prize. But Pyrocles, upon his release, put on poor clothes and engaged himself as servant to the executioner. Thus when Musidorus was on the scaffold, he was able to place a sword in his hand, and together they did great slaughter, which led to a mutiny against the tyrant, and finally to a battle in which he and his son were killed. Having placed a virtuous elderly member of the royal family on the throne, they passed on to Pontus, which was under the cruel rule of another tyrant, who was put to death on the tomb of two of his victims. Having further rid the Kingdom of two monstrous giants and established good government they set forth again.

Their next encounter is uniquely memorable not so much for its own sake as because it was destined to be adapted and immortalized by Shakespeare, and to prove that the *Arcadia* was known to him. They meet the blind King of Paphlagonia, led by his son Leonatus. The King tells that having had this son by a lawful marriage, he had afterwards had a bastard named Plexirtus, who had incited him to kill his true heir. The bastard had then assumed the royal prerogatives, leaving his father nothing but the name of a King, and had afterwards dispossessed him, put out his eyes, and sent him forth. Leonatus having escaped death, and hearing of this, had come to his father's aid, as a glass to his blind eyes. The King had begged him to lead him to the top of a rock, from which he would throw himself down, but for the first time

Leonatus had disobeyed him. Then Plexirtus had made another unsuccessful attempt on the life of his brother, and had been deserted by his subjects, whereupon the King had set the crown upon Leonatus, to whom he did fealty and thereupon died from a broken heart. Plexirtus having come in person to surrender obtained pardon from Leonatus.

Every reader of *King Lear* will recognize in the blind King and his two sons the prototypes of the Earl of Gloster and Edgar and Edmund in their mutual relationships, though at the close the romance and the play take somewhat different turns.

The next adventure of the Princes was the delivery from her agonizing dilemma of Queen Erona of Lycia. While still a young Princess she had persuaded the King, her father, to pull down and deface the statues and pictures of Cupid exhibited throughout the Kingdom. For this the god of love a year afterwards took his revenge. Erona fell obstinately in love with Antiphilus, a young man of mean birth, the son of her nurse. Her father sought to counter this by making a marriage between her and King Tiridates of Armenia, 'who desired her more than the joys of heaven'. To this end her father tried various devices, even pretending to execute Antiphilus. But when she thought that he was dead she attempted suicide, 'to send her soul at least to be married in the eternal church with him'. Upon her heart-broken father's death, as Queen she became her own mistress, and prepared to give her love for Antiphilus the holy title of matrimony. But before this could take place, Tiridates made war upon her, and, as though there could be found no foil to set forth the extremity of his love but extremity of hatred, wrote (as it were) the sonnets of his love in the blood, and tuned them in the cries, of her subjects. He besieged her in her chief city, vowing to win her or lose his life.

Then came to her rescue Pyrocles and Musidorus, who succeeded in entering the city, but were baulked of full victory by Plangus, cousin of Tiridates and General of his horsemen. In a duel proposed by Tiridates to shorten hostilities, Pyrocles and Musidorus slew their opponents, but Antiphilus was taken prisoner by Plangus, and was condemned by Tiridates to be beheaded on the third day following, unless Erona yields to his suit. The situation is in some ways akin to that of Angelo, Isabella and Claudio in *Measure for Measure*, but here Erona is in perplexity, portrayed by Sidney in dialogue form, which course to take. She sends a message to Tiridates accepting his condition for sparing the life of Antiphilus, and then immediately recanting, arranges with Pyrocles and Musidorus to sally forth from the city at dead of night, kill the King and deliver Antiphilus who soon afterwards was married to Erona, though against the consent of all her nobility. Thus summarily ends this phase of an exciting narrative.

But after Miso had recounted some memories of a good old woman's warning to her, when she was an admired pretty girl, and Mopsa had begun a ridiculous tale, Pamela, at her sister's request, added the story of Plangus to that of Erona. He was a Prince, the son of the King of Iberia by his first wife, who had died in his infancy. As a young man he had become enamoured of the wife of a private citizen. His misconduct with her was discovered by his father, who himself fell in love with the lady, and, to get rid of his younger rival, sent away Plangus with an army to subdue a rebellious distant province. The husband soon afterwards dying, the lady used all her arts to cajole the King into marrying her, and when Plangus came back victorious they had already two children. The Queen, feeling that his presence at Court was her condemnation, tried every means to excite her husband's suspicion and jealousy of him. Finally she induced the Iberian Parliament to persuade the aged King to make Plangus his associate in government. Though Plangus protested against this, the King thought he was merely dissembling and resolved to put him out of the way. But with the help of a number of faithful friends Plangus made his escape and took refuge with his cousin Tiridates. For many years he hoped in vain that his father would take him into grace again. But under the sway of his second wife the King hated him more and more, and caused Palladius, his son by this wife, to be proclaimed his successor and Plangus quite excluded.

# CHAPTER XVI

# PAMPHILUS AND DIDO –
# DEATHS OF PALLADIUS AND HIS MOTHER

Pamela was continuing her recital when Basilius suddenly appeared, and invited her hearers to follow the example of the setting sun and return to their lodgings. Then for a short time Sidney returns to the central theme of Zelmane, himself in love with Philoclea, being pestered by the amorous advances of Basilius and Gynecia. How effective are his homely parallels! 'Zelmane betwixt both (like the poor child, whose father, while he beats him, will make him believe it is for love; or like the sick man, to whom the physician swears the ill-tasting, wallowish[1] medicine he proffers is of a good taste) their love was hateful, their courting troublesome, their presence cause of her absence thence, where not only her light but her life consisted.' A crisis is reached when Basilius declares his passion for Zelmane as heavenly woman or earthly goddess, and begs her to 'look upon him with pity, whose life serves for your praise'. Zelmane takes advantage of this to tell him that these words spoken by Philoclea 'as by one woman to another' might have a more favourable reception. Basilius thereupon in fervid terms besought Philoclea to 'save his gray hairs from rebuke and his aged mind from despair', and 'by one payment requite all his deserts'. The girl eagerly took the opportunity of meeting Zelmane alone, and heard him declare that he was Pyrocles, Prince of Macedon, metamorphosed into an Amazon for love of her. Her answer assures him that his love is returned. 'Thou has then the victory: use it with virtue. Thy virtue won me; with virtue preserve me. Dost thou love me? Keep me then worthy to be beloved.'

Leaving the couple in each other's arms, and under promise of marriage, Sidney again goes off at a tangent by making Philoclea ask Pyrocles for an account of his adventures after the parting from Queen Erona. A nephew, Anaxius, of his

[1] Nauseous.

opponent killed by him in the combat on her behalf, a man
of valour but of overweening pride, had challenged him to
a duel in the confines of the Kingdom of Lycia. On his way
thither a strange happening had befallen him. In a thickly
wooded copse he had come across a gentleman bound hand
and foot whom nine gentlewomen, with bodkins in their
hands, were continually pricking. Pyrocles was about to
respond to his cries for help when a band of Knights rushed
up and forbade him to trouble the ladies, who were taking
their due revenge. Pyrocles slew some of them and put the
others to flight, whereupon the women ran away except one,
Dido by name. She explained that this man called Pamphilus,
very gifted and attractive, had won the affections of each of
these women, and then on various excuses had deserted them
in turn, in her case because there were many others fairer,
which she denied. Having at length pacified her Pyrocles
rode on to keep his engagement with Anaxius, but during
their hard-fought duel she again appeared on a palfrey,
followed by Pamphilus who was beating her with wands. In
spite of taunts of cowardice Pyrocles broke off the duel and
went to Dido's help. In return she invited him to stay the
night in the castle of her miserly father Chremes, 'a drivel-
ling old fellow, lean, shaking both of head and hands . . .
Who scarcely would give me thanks for that I had done for
fear, I suppose, that thankfulness might have an introduction
of reward.' On learning who Pyrocles was, he planned to
behead him, to secure the rich price set on his head by Queen
Artaxia, sister of Tiridates. But through the timely intervention of Musidorus and the King of Iberia the plot failed.
Chremes was hanged, and Dido seeking to protect Pyrocles
from her father's clowns met her death.

The two cousins had been wounded in the fray, and the
King of Iberia offered them the hospitality of his Court. He
was so completely under the sway of his imperious wife that
'he scarcely knew what was done in his own chamber, but
as it pleased her instruments to frame the relation'. She became enamoured of both the princes, and when they rejected
her advances, she accused them of plotting to overthrow the
King, who put them in prison. Their release came in unexpected fashion. By this queen the King had a young son,

Palladius, who had supplanted in popular affection his exiled half-brother, Plangus. He had fallen deeply in love with a lady at the Court, Zelmane.[1] But instead of returning his passion, she gave her affection to Pyrocles. To gratify Zelmane, Palladius took advantage of a special opportunity to set the prisoners free. On the anniversary of his marriage it was the King's custom to honour it with some public ceremony, of which a tournament was specially popular. On this occasion Helen, Queen of Corinth, had sent a number of choice Knights of her Court to contend for victory.

In this for the first three days they were successful, whereupon Palladius, for the recovery of the honour of the Iberian Court, obtained the Queen's leave for the Princes to fight alongside with him, on condition that they should keep with him, and not go beyond the appointed limits. It was not till the following afternoon that they took part in the combat, and both then and during the whole of the next day they carried off the honours. Then Palladius called to the Princes to follow him, and brought them to a little house in a forest nearby, where they could rest till they got further from his mother's fury. Though she followed them impetuously with a troop of horsemen she could not overtake them till they reached the Kingdom of Bythinia, out of her jurisdiction. Here a struggle took place in which Palladius was mortally wounded. His mother thereupon stabbed herself with his dagger, and Pyrocles ran to her aid. But, as he ends his recital to Philoclea, 'the wound was past the cure of a better surgeon than myself, so as I could but receive some few of her dying words, which were cursings on her ill-set affection, and wishing unto me every cross and mischances in my love whensoever I should love, wherein I fear, and only fear, that her prayer is from above granted'.

Journeying onwards they were overtaken by a young gentleman, as it seemed, who called himself Daiphantus, son of an Iberian nobleman, and asked to be taken into the service of Pyrocles. But the apparent page was no other than Zelmane, unrecognized in her disguise, and showing

there is no service like his that serves because he loves,

[1] It is unfortunate that Sidney should have given her the same name as that assumed by Pyrocles when posing as an Amazon.

for, though born of Prince's blood, brought up with tenderest education, unapt to service because a woman, and full of thoughts because in a strange estate, yet love enjoined such diligence that no apprentice, no, no bondslave could ever be by fear more ready at all commandments than that young Princess was . . . How often would she come creeping to me, between gladness to be near me, and fear to offend me!

But before long she was laid low by extreme sickness, and on her dying bed she revealed who she was. She begged Pyrocles to pardon her father Plexirtus for the wrongs he had done and go to his assistance: that when he came to Greece he would take the name of Daiphantus in memory of her, and Musidorus that of Palladius; and that she be buried obscurely till he returned to his own country, when her bones would be conveyed to some place there, 'which he would sometimes vouchsafe to visit'. Thus the real Zelmane disappears from the *Arcadia* where she is a short-lived but appealing figure.

# CHAPTER XVII

# POLITICAL DEBATE – QUEEN ERONA

Pyrocles then tells of his further adventures till the ship-wreck, of which he gives a vividly detailed account, which parted him for a time from Musidorus.

The discourse between him and Philoclea was interrupted by Miso, acting on behalf of Gynecia, to whom she returned with the news that 'her daughter had been a whole hour together in secret talk with Zelmane'. Then, as in the original version, Gynecia came after them and sending Philoclea home, 'began to display to Zelmane the storehouse of her deadly desires' till she was silenced by the cries of the mutinous multitude. By the prowess of the two disguised Princes, aided by Basilius, the rebels, of whom some grimly grotesque particulars are now given, were put to rout. Then Zelmane went forth boldly to parley with the rebels, and told them that the Duke wished them to choose someone who would report their grievances to him. Here once again Sidney showed his distrust of the popular voice.

Never bees made such a confused humming, the town-dwellers demanding putting down of imposts, the coun-try-fellows laying out of commons. Some would have the Prince keep his Court in one place, some in another. All cried out to have new councillors, but when they should think of any new, they liked them as well as any other that they could remember; especially they would have the treasurer so looked into as that he would never need to take any more subsidies. At length they fell to discreet contrarieties. For the artisans, they would have corn and wine set at a lower price, and bound to be kept so still; the ploughmen, vine-labourers and farmers would none of that. The countrymen demanded that every man might be free in the chief towns: that could not the burgesses like of. The peasants would have the gentlemen destroyed: the citizens (especially such as cooks, barbers and those others that lived most on gentlemen) would but have them reformed. And of each side were like divisions, one neighbour beginning to find fault with another.

They could not even agree upon a spokesman to the Duke, whereupon Zelmane, asking, 'If you cannot agree upon one to speak for you, how can you agree upon one to fight for you?', offered on his behalf a free pardon to all who would turn their weapons to protect him. The majority accepted the offer, but amongst them was a crafty fellow Clinias, not mentioned in the original version, who played a hypocritical part. And here Sidney makes one of his most interesting theatrical references, on the evil effect in some cases of acting in academic plays.

> This Clinias in his youth had been a scholar so far as to learn rather words than manners, and of words rather plenty than order; and oft had used to be an actor in tragedies, where he had learned, besides a slidingness of language, acquaintance with many passions, and to frame his face to bear the figure of them; long used to the eyes and ears of men; and to reckon no fault but shamefastness.

He had stirred up the rebels, but seeing that their fury had begun to ebb, he urged them to submit themselves to their good Prince, their good Basilius. A farmer, 'disdaining that this fellow should play the preacher, who had been one of the chiefest make-hates', struck him in the face with his sword, whereupon a general melée began, in which many were killed and about a score fled to the woods. After another oration by Clinias, the Duke, 'that was not the sharpest piercer into masked minds, took a good liking to him', and sent him home to be cured of his wound.

Basilius was next employed in relating to Zelmane by request the further story of Erona, Queen of Lycia, and her low-born husband, Antiphilus. It was not long after their marriage that he showed that his conception of sovereignty was to do what he liked, and make 'his kingdom a tennis-court where his subjects should be the balls'. He even made an 'unlawful law', permitting more than one wife, and while keeping Erona, asked in marriage Artaxia, Queen of

Armenia. She pretended acceptance, but when he and Erona, who had consented to be a second-place wife, arrived for a solemn conference, Artaxia, in revenge for the death of her brother Tiridates, put them into irons, purposing to sacrifice them on his tomb. But Plangus, the cousin of Artaxia, fell in love with Erona, and sought to deliver her, but she only begged him for her sake to save Antiphilus. Reluctantly he planned this, but Antiphilus, in the hope of a pardon, revealed the plot. It was then agreed that, unless Erona was delivered by the victory of two Knights over Pyrocles and Musidorus on the day two years after the death of Tiridates, she was to die by burning. Meanwhile Artaxia had married Plexirtus, who was crowned King of Armenia. Plangus had no other resource than to betake himself to Euarchus, the powerful and good King of Macedonia. At this point of the Duke's narrative Zelmane, assured that Euarchus would deliver Erona and to prevent any further declaration of love by Basilius, let the shepherds begin the performance of their eclogues.

Sidney then returns to Musidorus, who encouraged by some kind words of Pamela presumes to take her in his arms and offers to kiss her. But she repels him disdainfully and bade him see her no more. He fled for two days into the woods, 'disdaining to give his body food, or his mind comfort, loving in himself nothing but the love of her'. Then he summoned up courage to write to her and have the fears and doubts of a nervous correspondent ever been more vividly described?

> Never pen did more quakingly perform his office; never was paper more double nourished with ink and tears; never words more slowly married together . . . This word was not significant; that word was too plain; this would not be conceived; the other would be ill conceived; here sorrow was not enough expressed, there he seemed for his own sake to be sorry . . . At last, marring with mending, and putting out better than he left, he made an end of it.

It was an epistle in verse which he placed in a standish in her chamber, begging for pity, and bidding 'long farewell' to 'all my woe, all my delight'. Here Pamela found it, and after much hesitation read it, but before she could decide how to act upon it she was called down to help to entertain Zelmane. By a trick, however, the two sisters, with Zelmane and Miso, were decoyed into the power of their evil aunt-in-law Cecropia. By the marriage of Basilius at the age of seventy years to Gynecia and the birth of their two daughters, her expectation that her son Amphialus would succeed to the throne of Arcadia had been defeated. Her attempts to destroy the Duke and his family by savage beasts and by mutineers had failed, and as Amphialus had fallen in love with Philoclea she had now entrapped the girl for him, 'yet wishing hate rather than love in you'. He at once dressed in his best, went to her chamber, and besought her to take what was done in good part, as there was nothing but honour meant unto her person, and in her hands the balance of his life or death did stand. But she answered, 'What shall my tongue be able to do, which is informed by the ears one way, and by the eyes another? You call for pity and use cruelty: you say you love me, and yet do the effects of cruelty.' To which Amphialus retorts, 'It is love, not I which disobey you . . . I am not the stay of your freedom, but love, love, which ties you in your own knots.' All his persuasions failing, his mother undertakes to plead for him with her 'sweet niece', whose vow that she will lead a virgin's life she counters with a picture of the joys of the married state. But neither this nor serenades by night nor presents by day prevailed with Philoclea, whereupon Cecropia bethought herself of attempting the no less beautiful Pamela. On listening at her door she heard her breathing forth the fervent prayer which Milton was later to reproach Charles I with using:

O all-seeing Light and Eternal Life of all things, to whom nothing is either so great that it may resist, or so small that it is contemned, look upon my misery, and let thine infinite power vouchsafe to limit out some proportion of deliverance unto me, as to thee shall seem most convenient. Let not injury, O Lord, triumph over me, and let my faults by thy hands be corrected, and make not mine unjust enemy the minister of thy will. But yet, my God, if in thy wisdom this be the aptest chastisement for my inexcusable folly; if this low bondage be fittest for my over high desires; if the pride of my not-enough humble heart be thus to be broken, O Lord, I yield unto thy will, and joyfully embrace what sorrow thou wilt have me suffer.

It would have been a proud satisfaction to Sidney could he have known that these words would fit so aptly the lips of a succession of his sovereigns.

# CHAPTER XVIII

# CECROPIA'S CASTLE – HER PLOTS FOR AMPHIALUS

Again Crecopia's attempts at persuasion failed, and they were cut short by the arrival at her castle of the army of Basilius led by Philanax to rescue the besieged prisoners. There follows a detailed account of the conflict, and especially of the valiant deeds of Amphialus, who takes Philanax prisoner, but, at the intercession of Philoclea, sets him free. Cecropia in vain seeks to make capital out of this, and then again turns to Pamela, exclaiming, 'Beauty, beauty, dear niece, is the crown of the feminine greatness: which gift on whomsoever the heavens (therein most niggardly) do bestow, without question she is bound to use it to the noble purpose for which it is created.' Pamela retorts that God claims her obedience to her father, who has refused all offers for her hand. Cecropia counters this with a derisively sceptical argument: 'to think that those powers (if there be any such) above are moved either by the eloquence of our prayers, or in a chafe at the folly of our actions, carries as much reason as if flies should think men take great care which of them hums sweetest, and which of them flies nimblest.'

At this point Pamela burst in, 'Peace, wicked woman, peace! unworthy to breathe that dost not acknowledge the Breath-giver; most unworthy to have a tongue, which speaketh against Him, through whom thou speakest.' And thereupon Pamela launches forth into what must be the most singular of replies by a maiden to a plea that she should be wedded. But it is to be valued as a statement of Sidney's own philosophic position, and should be read as a whole. Here are some salient points:

> This godly work of which we are, and in which we live, hath not his being by chance; on which opinion it is beyond marvel by what chance any brain could stumble. For if it be eternal, as you would seem to conceive of it,

eternity and chance are things insufferable together . . .

This world therefore cannot otherwise consist but by a mind of wisdom which governs it; which whether you will allow to be the Creator thereof, as undoubtedly He is, or the Soul and Governor thereof, most certain it is that whether He govern all or make all, His power is above either His creatures or His government. And if His power be above all things, then consequently it must needs be infinite, since there is nothing above it to limit it.

Even the formidable Cecropia was for the time overcome and after Pamela's speech rather muttered than replied. So the narrative is switched off again to feats of arms. The youthful Phalantus of Corinth having been overthrown by Amphialus, Basilius invokes the aid of Argalus, who answers the call in spite of the protests of his newly wedded bride Parthenia. Between him and Amphialus, after both had been unhorsed, took place 'the cruellest combat that any present eye had seen', till it was halted by Parthenia flinging herself between them. It was too late to save Argalus, though her kisses made him happy as he died.

Then to tragic pathos succeeds comic relief. Dametas, who is in the camp of Basilius, hearing Clinias dubbed a coward sends him a provocative challenge which is not at once accepted. Thereupon Dametas, taking delay for a denial, 'began to speak his loud voice, to look big, to march up and down, and in his march to lift his legs higher than he was wont, swearing, by no mean devotions, that the walls should not keep the coward from him, but he would fetch him out of his coney-burrow'. But on the next day Clinias, spurred on by Amphialus, replied that if Dametas appeared he would cut him to pieces, joint by joint. Then follows a duel in which both combatants engage as reluctantly as Sir Andrew Aguecheek and Viola in *Twelfth Night*. But at length Dametas, with his experience of the flail, gets Clinias down and cries that he will save him if he throws away his sword. When Clinias obeyed he treacherously prepared to cut his throat till the judges intervened and told him that he was breaking the law of arms. But Clinias, thus saved, was guilty of worse treachery. He conspired with Artesia, Cecropia's leading lady-in-waiting, to open the castle gates to the besiegers, and to poison Amphialus, and thus to liberate the princesses, to whom they revealed the plot. But both of them indignantly refused to gain their freedom by such means, and after Artesia's confession to Cecropia she was locked up in her chamber and Clinias was executed.

Then another outstanding figure appeared on the scene, the famous prince Anaxius, proudest of the proud, with his two brothers, and two hundred chosen horsemen, with whom he thought himself able to conquer the world. He had fought four times on equal terms with Amphialus, but on one occasion had saved his life and won his friendship. Amphialus gave him welcome and entertainment, but he cared only for combat, and put the forces of Basilius to rout till there came to their support three Knights of whom the one in black armour gave challenge to Amphialus. Before they could meet, another strange Knight appeared, with four damsels riding on palfreys in front, and four behind, all apparelled in mourning weeds, and himself in armour so painted as to represent a gaping sepulchre. This Knight of the tomb, as the soldiers called him, also sent by one of his gentlewomen a challenge to Amphialus which he reluctantly accepted. Victor in the duel he pulled off the strange Knight's helmet, only to find from her golden hair and lovely face that it was no other than Parthenia. Kneeling down beside her he protested his life and power to be ready to do her honour. With her dying breath Parthenia murmured:

Sir, I pray you, if prayers have place in enemies, to let my maids take my body untouched by you: the only honour I now desire by your means is that I have no honour of you. Argalus made no such bargain with you that the hands which killed him should help me. I have of them (and I do not only pardon you but thank you for it) the service which I desired. There rests nothing now but that I go live with him since whose death I have done nothing but die. . . . I come, my Argalus, I come: and, O God, hide my faults in thy mercies, and grant, as I feel thou dost grant, that in thy eternal love, we may love each other eternally. And this, O Lord—

Here the wished-for death cut her words short. With her gentlewomen mourning, and Basilius himself helping to carry her, she was brought to a church a mile from the camp, and laid beside her Argalus, with two marble images to represent them, and with this epitaph:

> They joy'd one joy: one grief they griev'd;
> One love they lov'd: one life they liv'd . . .
> As all the rest, so now the stone
> That tombs the two is justly one.

From this touching episode it is a harsh transition to Cecropia, urging the sorrow-stricken Amphialus to use force instead of persuasion in gaining possession of Philoclea, and quoting the examples of Hercules and Paris. But before he could answer there came another challenge from one who called himself 'the forsaken Knight', who would bring two other Knights with him: Amphialus met him, with the two brothers of Anaxius. A long description follows of the encounter between the equally matched champions. 'Never game of death better played: never fury set itself forth in greater bravery.' Both performed prodigies of valour and were so sorely wounded that they had to be carried off the field by their allies. But both were frustrated in their aims – the forsaken Knight (none other than Musidorus) because he could not rescue Pamela, and Amphialus because he could not prove himself victor in the sight of Philoclea.

Cecropia then threatened that unless Basilius raised the siege she would cause the heads of the three prisoners to be cut off before his eyes. Urged by Gynecia he yielded, but would not agree to her further demand that he should give his daughter in marriage to her son. Cecropia then had recourse to every extremity. With the aid of certain wicked old women she beat Philoclea with a rod till she begged for death. 'It is no great suit to an enemy when but death is desired, I crave but that.' Instead of granting her request Cecropia used the same cruelty to Pamela, equally in vain. Then taking counsel of one of the wicked old women she told Philoclea that 'now she was to come to the last part of the play . . . she was now minded that one of their deaths should serve for an example to the other – she would begin

with her sister who that afternoon should have had her head
cut off before her face, if in the meantime one of them did
not pull out their ill-wrought stitches of unkindness'.

In vain Philoclea pleaded that she should be the victim,
and she saw the apparent execution of her sister, for whom
she lamented as David for Jonathan. And this was followed
by an exhibition of the dissevered head of Philoclea to
Pyrocles, the supposed Zelmane, who moaned, 'Philoclea is
dead, and yet life is not ashamed to continue upon the earth.
Philoclea is dead. O deadly word, which containeth in itself
the uttermost of all misfortune. But happy word when thou
shalt be said of me, and long it shall not be before it be said.'
But neither of the sisters had really suffered death. It was
Artesia, dressed in Pamela's clothes, who had been executed,
and it was by a trick with a golden bowl whose bottom had
been beaten out that Philoclea had seemed to be beheaded.
When news of their evil treatment came to Amphialus he
rose in spite of his wounds, and snatching a sword from one
of his servants went in search of his mother who had betaken
herself to the leads of the roof. His intention was to kill himself in her presence, but thinking that he meant to strike her
with his sword, she flung herself over the leads 'to receive
her death's kiss at the ground'.

To Amphialus it was the last straw that he should be the
cause of his mother's death, and with a knife that had been
Philoclea's he gave himself a mortal wound, crying to her,
'Unworthy I am, unhappy I am, false I am; but to thee alas!
I am not false.' It is scarcely heroic enough an exit for one
who has so long filled the centre of the stage, pushing
Pyrocles and Musidorus into the background. To bring it
more closely home to his readers Sidney stresses the furious
grief of his friend Anaxius, and the distress of Queen Helen
who had so long sought him, only to be sorry to find him,
and who now carried him to her own country to have him
buried under monuments fit for her love and his worthiness.

After this it is an anti-climax to find Anaxius and his
brothers seeking to win by force the possession of the Princesses and the supposed Zelmane who, having killed the
brothers, became engaged in a long-drawn duel with Anaxius. 'The Irish greyhound against the English mastiff; the

sword-fish against the whale; the rhinoceros against the elephant, might be models, and but models of this combat.'

It was in the description of this encounter that a chasm was occasioned 'by the loss of some of the Author's invaluable papers', which was first supplied by Sir William Alexander, afterwards Earl of Stirling, as a 'Supplement of a defect in the third part of this History' in a Dublin edition of the *Arcadia* in 1621, and in a London edition in 1623. The Supplement relates the close of the duel in which Zelmane, though grievously wounded, is the victor, and is recognized as Pyrocles by the black Knight as Musidorus. Whilst they are embracing and the sight of Musidorus is lending strength to his stricken friend, a false report of Zelmane's death spreads through the castle and reaches the ladies' ears. It prostrates Philoclea with grief, and she is revealing the secret of her love for him when he enters and she finds herself in his arms. As she and Pamela praise his valour in delivering them, he points to the black Knight, exclaiming 'there is the deliverer of us all'. As he lowers his helmet Pamela recognizes Musidorus, and is inwardly overjoyed; but 'borrowing a mask from hate wherewith to hide love', chided him for breaking into her presence and said 'that she would not Dametas to lose a servant nor Mopsa a suitor by her means; and if he would needs return towards the lodges that he should first expect some employment homewards from her'. From his hint of service for her Musidorus took much comfort, but his love of Pyrocles detained him for a time at the castle. Here the chance discovery that they occupied one bed aroused the jealousy of Pamela, and forced the blushing Philoclea to reveal to her that 'Zelmane is the Prince Pyrocles, he whom you have heard so oft, yet ever to his honour, named; and, to define him to you particularly, the friend of Musidorus over whom with him you are jealous.'

The false report of Zelmane's death plunged both Basilius and Gynecia in misery till they learned the truth, when Gynecia sent him a sovereign balm for his wounds to be used when he was alone, and Basilius ordered Philanax to invite him back to the lodge as soon as he could be moved. On the morrow they all set forth and were welcomed on their way by Basilius and at the lodge by Gynecia, each specially singling out Zelmane. Even Dametas came leaping to meet Pamela, 'swearing that he had ventured more for her than he would do for all the world again, and for his own life too'; and complaining of the cowardice of his man Dolrus, who had disappeared, but had now sent word that he was driving home some ewes that had strayed. To which Pamela replied, 'He may be an evil soldier, but yet a good shepherd; and I hope that you keep him that he may keep sheep, not that he may kill men.' 'I may well chide the fellow,' admitted Dametas, 'but I will not beat him.'

Then with a graphic picture of the company sitting at supper the supplement closes.

# CHAPTER XIX

# THE 'ARCADIA' THROUGH THE CENTURIES
## – THE TWO VERSIONS COMPARED

It is at this point that in the folio of 1593 the narrative continues with the return of Basilius and his daughters to the
lodges and thenceforward follows in the main the original
version, supplied from a manuscript in the possession of the
Countess of Pembroke. Thus the *Arcadia* in the form in
which it reached its wide public in the 1593 and 1598 folios
and subsequent editions for more than three centuries was a
composite structure, on two levels, but this was unsuspected
not only by general readers but by critics. In 1599 an edition
was published in Edinburgh, followed by one in London in
1605, and another in 1615. A Dublin edition in 1621 contained, as noted above, Sir W. Alexander's Supplement to
the Book III, which appeared in the subsequent London
editions, 1623, 1627, 1629, the last of which included an
introductory sixth Book by R. B[eling] of Lincoln's Inn,
reproduced in the 1635 and 1638 editions. The 1655, 1662
and 1674 editions added a 'Life and death' of Sidney and a
'brief table of the principal Heads'.

Thus its popularity survived the Civil War and the Re-
storation till it was successfully challenged first by the vogue
of the French romances and then by the novels of Richard-
son, Fielding and their successors in the eighteenth century.
But thereafter the place of the many who had read the
*Arcadia* for entertainment was taken by the more select few
who found in it material for critical discussion. As has been
seen, the trail had been blazed by Abraham Fraunce in his
*The Arcadian Rhetorike*, where he had taken eighty illustrations from the old *Arcadia*. About ten years later John
Hoskyns in his manuscript *Directions for Speech and Style*
(B. M. Harl. 460) gave an elaborate technical analysis of the
various devices and figures of speech in the 1590 edition of

the new *Arcadia*. A valuable summary of this was provided by Miss Mona Wilson.[1]

The novelist, Jane Porter, opened the nineteenth-century references with two volumes in 1807 of *Aphorisms of Sir Philip Sidney, Remarks*. An article in *The Retrospective Review* (1820), stating in extravagant terms the superiority of the style of the *Arcadia* over Euphuism, was probably by James Crossley whose name was attached to its almost identical reproduction in book form in 1853. But the serious comparison of 'Arcadiaism' and Euphuism had to wait till the publications of Friedrich Landmann on the latter in 1881–7, in which he showed the debt of Lyly to the Spaniard, Antonio de Guevara.

In 1891 H. Oskar Sommer provided 300 copies of a photographic facsimile of the 1590 quarto, with a bibliographical introduction on the various early editions of the *Arcadia*. W. W. (now Sir Walter) Greg in a section of his *Pastoral Poetry and Pastoral Drama* (1906) gave an account of seven plays based on the romance, apart from the blinded Gloster episode in *King Lear*. Four of these are founded on the main plot of Basilius and the fortunes of his family. They include two published plays, John Day's *Isle of Gulls* (1605) and James Shirley's *Arcadia* (1640), together with two manuscripts, *Love's Changeling's Change*, in British Museum Egerton MS. 1994, and *The Arcadian Lovers, or the Metamorphosis of Princes* (Bodley Rawlinson, Part 3). Three other plays dramatize episodic stories in the revised *Arcadia*. They are Beaumont and Fletcher's *Cupid's Revenge* (1615) for Erona's defiances of him; *Andromara* by J.S. (1660) on the same subject, and *Argalus and Parthenia* by Henry Glapthorne (1639).

As to the *Arcadia's* own sources Hoskyns had started the hunt by declaring that they were Heliodorus in Greek, Sannazaro's *Arcadia* in Italian, and Montemayor's *Diana* in Spanish. S. L. Wolfe, in *The Greek Romances in Elizabethan Prose Fiction* (1912), added to the influence of Heliodorus in his *Theaginets and Chariclea* that of the later romance writer, Achilles Tatius of Alexandria, in his *Leudippe and Clitophon*. Other Greek influence on the *Arcadia*, especially that of

[1] Op. cit., pp. 304–9.

Aristotle, is claimed to an exaggerated degree by Friedrich Brie in his *Sidney's 'Arcadia', Eine Studie zur englischen Renaissance*.

Of the two other sources mentioned by Hoskyns, Sannazaro gave Sidney little more than the name of his romances. Montemayor's *Diana* resembled the English *Arcadia*, especially in its revised version, in its looseness of structure and its medley of incidents, but none of these are alike in the two romances. But Hoskyns omitted what seems to have been a more important influence on Sidney's work, the French *Amadis de Gaule*, which he had incidentally mentioned in the *Defence of Poesie*. It is to an American scholar, William Vaughan Moody, that we owe the discovery of the parallelism of a number of features in the *Amadis de Gaule* and the *Arcadia*. R. W. Zandvoort has had access to the contents of Moody's unpublished prize essay on *The Sources of Sir Philip Sidney's 'Arcadia'*, deposited in the Harvard library, and has given a summary of its chief conclusions.[1]

The purely textual reproduction of the *Arcadia* was notably advanced by Feuillerat's 1912 edition of the 1590 quarto, with its variants till 1674, in Volume I of *The Complete Works of Sir Philip Sidney*. This was followed in 1922 by a similar edition in Volume II of the additional Books from the 1593 folio. Meanwhile the epoch-making article of Bertram Dobell, 'New Light on Sidney's *Arcadia*', in *The Quarterly Review*, July 1909, revealing the existence in manuscript of the Old *Arcadia*, had been the prelude to a new departure in criticism of the romance. But this was necessarily limited in scope till Feuillerat printed the original version in Volume IV of his edition (1926). Hence has arisen a controversy on its merits as compared with the later version. It is something of a paradox that Dobell, who first realized the significance of the manuscript copies, gave them the preference in his *Quarterly Review* article, while Feuillerat, who first made this form of the romance available in print, described it as 'certainly inferior in literary value to the revised form published in 1590', and 'the immature work of a young man of great promise who is trying his hand at romance writing'.

[1] Op. cit., pp. 189–95. See further Zandvoort's detailed Bibliography, pp. 200–15.

To judge by the number of editions through which the revised version quickly went, it certainly found favour with Elizabethan and Stuart readers, and became what in modern parlance would be termed a 'best-seller'. But twentieth-century critics for the most part have sided, though with some qualification, with Dobell in preferring the old *Arcadia*. An important exception is Zandvoort who rates the new version more highly, as showing an advance in Sidney's powers of characterization and narrative.[1] In its straight-forward structure the original had much of the effect of a five-act play, with sufficient variety provided by the humorous underplot of Dametas and his family. I am in general agreement with this view. But it seems to have occurred to Sidney that his sister and her coterie of friends wanted more diversified entertainment, and he thus proceeded to interweave with his original design a series of what I have called novelettes which have little or no connexion with it; or which involve chronological confusion. Nor are these additions, as in the case of some well-known novels of a later date, in the form of narrative insertions. They are usually put into the mouth of one of the characters and are liable to interruption by the entrance of another, and may, or may not, be resumed after an interval. Thus is created a fictional labyrinth in which it is difficult to keep track always of Queen Helen of Corinth or Queen Erona, and where Queen Cecropia and Amphialus thrust what are the leading characters too long into the background. Moreover what has been from the beginning a mannered style tends to become somewhat monotonously overloaded in this extended fashion.

So far for the debit side of the revised *Arcadia*. But even in respect of style it includes, as has been seen, some of Sidney's most masterly descriptive and narrative passages. It also gives additional proof of his skill in character-drawing, sometimes on a minute scale, and in analysing emotions. But what I would suggest, has not been sufficiently noted by the partisans of either of the versions is the important light thrown by the additions on Sidney's personal interests and attainments. This is particularly true of the similes which are so constant a feature of his technique. That he should show

[1] Op. cit., especially Chaps. 2 and 3.

himself familiar with the details of masculine attire, especially of armour in battle or tournament, was only to be expected. But he must have made a special appeal to the Countess of Pembroke and other fair ladies in his expert description of feminine headdress and costume. He had an equally observant eye for nature in her wilder aspects and when cultivated by the hand of man. And what is more surprising, he displayed a seaman's knowledge of the moods of the sea, both in storm and in calm. He showed acquaintance with something of the technique of the fine arts – architecture, sculpture, painting and music, and of the roles of the divine, and the doctor. And though his only legacy to the stage was the minor one of *The Lady of May* he was keenly interested in the problems and influence of the theatre, professional and amateur. With his academic trappings still clinging to him he might almost have claimed to have anticipated, within Elizabethan limits, Francis Bacon's boast that he had taken all knowledge to be his province.

# CHAPTER XX

# METRICAL VIRTUOSITY – PHILISIDES AND MIRA

In the foregoing attempt to give the outline of the *Arcadia* in its two versions I have almost entirely omitted the songs sung occasionally by the characters in the romance, mostly taking the form of the eclogues contributed by the shepherds in the pastoral festivities of which the Duke was patron. It may broadly be said that Sidney had too fastidious a taste for any of his poetic efforts to fall below a reputable level. Also, as the over-seer of the 1590 quarto testified, he had not made his final selection of them. Yet it must be admitted that few of them have established a claim to a place in Elizabethan anthologies.

There are, however, two groups which merit special notice, the one on metrical, the other on personal, grounds. A number of the eclogues gave Sidney the opportunity of showing his virtuosity in experimenting in both rhymed and unrhymed verse. Same examples may be given. In both versions of the first series of eclogues Lalus, accounted one of the best singers among the shepherds, challenges Dorus to celebrate their mistresses in song. Through a dozen stanzas in *terza rima*, remarkable for trisyllabic rhymes, each answers the other. Lalus extols his shepherdess Kala.

> Muse, hold your peace! but thou, my God Pan, glorify
> My Kala's gifts, who with all good gifts fillèd is;
> Thy pipe, O Pan, shall help, though I sing sorely.
> A heap of sweetness she is, where nothing spillèd is,
> Who though she be no bee, yet full of honey is:
> A lily field, with plough of rose which tillèd is;
> Mild as a lamb, more dainty than a coney[1] is.

Dorus retorts with praise of Pamela, though he does not venture to give her name.

[1] Rabbit.

Such Kala is, but ah! my fancies raisèd be
In one, whose name to name were high presumption,
Since virtues all to make her title pleasèd be.
O happy Gods which by inward assumption
Enjoy her soul, in body's fair possession,
And keep it joined, fearing your seats consumption.

Sidney was hard put to it to furnish Lalus' with a rhyme in
the opening of his next stanza.

How oft my doleful sire cried to me, 'tarry, son',
When first he spied my love, how oft he said to me
'Thou art no soldier fit for Cupid's garrison.'

Suddenly each of the disputants delivered himself in sixteen
lines of blank verse, followed by six stanzas of which the
peculiar feature is that the last line of each stanza sung by
Lalus is repeated by Dorus as the first of his. If the listeners
desired variety of technique, it is natural that they gave this
eclogue great commendation.

The next eclogue, in the 1590 version, sung by a melancholy young shepherd, was in seven-lined stanzas and tells
a strange tale. There was a time when beasts alone dwelt
on the earth and 'like senators a nameless empire had'. But
they besought Jove to let them have a King, and though he
warned them that 'rulers will think all things made them to
please', he offers to lend them part of his heavenly fire, while
they must give the rest. Each beast made his appropriate
contribution. 'Thus Man was made, thus Man their Lord
became,' and at first he treated the beasts as his equals,

Not in his sayings saying 'I', but 'we',
As if he meant his lordship common be.

But when he felt himself firmly placed he became despotic,
and used the beasts only for his own purposes, which provokes the rebuke:

But yet, O Man, rage not beyond thy need.
Deem it no glory to swell in tyranny.

An old shepherd, Geron, turns the listeners' thoughts into
a very different channel, by his praise of matrimony to
another young shepherd, Histor, who has been jilted by

Kala in favour of Lalus, and grown into a detester of marriage. One would wish to think that Sidney was speaking of his own experience with Frances Walsingham in these words.

> Believe me, man, there is no greater bliss
> Than is the quiet joy of loving wife,
> Which whoso wants, half of himself doth miss.
> Friend without change, playfellow without strife;
> Food without fulness; counsel without pride,
> In that sweet doubling of our single life.

Histor retorts that if there were many Kalas in Arcadia he would follow the example of Lalus, but most wives contribute to the home

> Either dull silence, or eternal chat:
> Still contrary to what her husband says:
> If he do praise the dog, she likes the cat:
> Austere she is, when he would honest plays.

Geron returns to the attack by declaring that it is a man's duty to take risks, and by pointing to his own example.

> Who only sees the ill is worse than blind.
> These fifty winters married have I been,
> And yet find no such faults in womankind.
>
> *          *          *
>
> And yet in all this time between us tway[1]
> We bear our double yoke with such consent
> That never passed foul word, I dare well say.

This is followed by a love-lorn duet composed by Strephon and Klaius in twelve six-line stanzas, each of which repeats in different order the same unrhymed dissyllabic word. Thus Strephon laments:

> I that was once free-burgess of the forests,
> Where shade from sun, and sports I sought at evening;
> I that was once esteem'd for pleasant music,
> Am vanished now among the monstrous mountains
> Of huge despair, and foul affliction's valleys,
> Am grown a shriek-owl to myself each morning.

[1] Twain.

This is echoed by Klaius:

> I that was once delighted every morning,
> Hunting the wild inhabiters of forests:
> I that was once the music of their valleys,
> So darkened am that all my day is evening,
> Heart-broken so, that molehills seem high mountains,
> And fill the vales with cries instead of music.

The festivities are concluded by Pyrocles (as Zelmane), with his eyes fixed on Philoclea singing a song addressed to Hope in Sapphic metre. The first stanza, repeated at the close, runs:

> If mine eyes can speak to do hearty errand,
> Or mine eyes' language she do hap to judge of,
> So that eyes' message be of her receivèd,
>     Hope, we do live yet.

Followed by:

> But if eyes fail then, when I most do need them,
> Or if eyes' language be not unto her known,
> So that eyes' message do return rejected,
>     Hope, we do both die.
> Yet dying, and dead, do we sing her honour;
> So become our tombs monuments of her praise;
> So becomes our loss the triumph of her gain:
>     Hers is the glory.

The series of eclogues at the close of Book II begins with a dialogue between a group of shepherds representing Reason and another representing Passion. The leader of the first group sings:

> Thou Rebel vile, come, to thy master yield,

to which his opposite number retorts,

> No, tyrant, no; mine, mine shall be the field.

They interchange for a time taunts in rhyming couplets till at last they embrace, singing together:

> Then let us both to heavenly rules give place,
> Which Passions kill and Reason do deface.

Then Dicus asks Dorus if his silence means 'Thy saint is dead, or dead is thy devotion?' If not, let him tell them

> how she was, how now she framéd is
>     To help, or hurt in thee her own infection.
> *Dorus:* Blest be the name, wherewith my mistress naméd is:
>     Whose wounds are salves, whose yokes please more
>                                     than pleasure doth.
>     Her stains are beams; virtue the fault she blaméd is,
>     The heart, eye, ear here only find his treasure doth.
>     All numbering arts her endless graces number not:
>     Time, place, life, wit scarcely her rare gifts measure
>                                                     doth.
>     Is she in rage? So is the sun in summer hot,
>     Yet harvest brings. Doth she, alas, absent herself?
>     The sun is hid; his kindly shadows cumber not.

It will be seen that Sidney has here returned to his favourite *terza rima*, and his trisyllabic rhymes which for no apparent reason he discards for about two dozen lines, and then resumes them in the final tribute of Dorus to his loved one:

> The quiet mind (whereof myself impairer is,
> As thou dost think) should most of all disquiet me
> Without her love, than any mind who fairer is,
> Her only cure for surfeit woes can diet me:
> She holds the balance of my concentration
> Her clearèd eyes, nought else, in storms can quiet me.

Then two jolly younkers, Nico and Pas, sing in praise of their mistresses, Leuca and Cosma, with Dicus as judge between them. They reach their peak in the following stanzas:

> *Nico:* O, if I had a ladder for the skies,
>     I would climb up, and bring a pretty star
>     To wear upon her neck, that open lies.
> *Pas:* O, if I had Apollo's golden car,
>     I would come down, and yield to her my place
>     That, shining now, she then might shine more far.
> *Nico:* Nothing, O Leuca, shall thy fame deface,
>     While shepherds' tunes be heard, or rhymes be read,
>     Or while those shepherds love a lovely face.

*Pas:* Thy name, O Cosma, shall with praise be spread,
 As far as any shepherd's piping be:
 As far as Love possesseth any head.

But the surly Dicus is not satisfied, and cries 'Enough, enough! so ill hath done the best.'

 Another set, on personal grounds, calls for special notice. Under the thin disguise of 'Philisides' Philip Sidney several times introduces himself as a woe-begone rejected lover. While the first eclogues are being performed an old shepherd, Geron, bending over a young one 'named Philisides', who neither had danced nor sung with them and had all this time lain upon the ground at the foot of a cypress tree (leaning upon his elbow with so deep a melancholy that his senses carried to his mind no delights from any of their objects), urged him:

 Up, up, Philisides, let sorrows pass.
 Who yields to woe, doth but increase his smart.

After replying for a time to the greybeard's exhortations, Philisides bursts forth impatiently:

 O Gods, how long this old fool hath annoyed
 My wearied ears! O Gods, yet grant me this,
 That soon the world of his false tongue be void.

In the second set of eclogues Basilius himself calls upon Philisides[1] sitting in his customary melancholy to entertain them. He began an eclogue between himself and the Echo, stressing the words to which he wished Echo to reply. Here are two of the hexameters, with the refrain:

 What medicine may I find for a pain that draws me to
  death? *Echo:* Death.
 In what state was I then when I took this deadly
  disease? *Echo:* Ease.

 At the close of the third Book in the original version Philisides does not appear in person, but Pyrocles recovering from his swoon repeats to Philoclea a song which he had

---

[1] In the old *Arcadia* his name is given; in the new version he is merely 'the young melancholy shepherd'.

heard Philisides sing 'of the beauties of his unkind mistress, which begins,

> What tongue can her perfections tell
> In whose each part all pens may dwell?

Through twenty stanzas he extols each part of her beauties in almost anatomical detail, ending with the fanciful conceits:

> Of whose high praise and praiseful bliss
> Goodness the pen, Heaven paper is,
> The Ink immortal fame doth lend.

In the old *Arcadia* among the fourth set of eclogues, when the shepherds are lamenting the supposed death of Basilius, they begged Philisides to impart to them some part of the sorrow his countenance well witnessed to them. He tells them:

> I was born of such parentage as neither left me so great that I was a mark of envy, nor so base that I was subject to contempt, brought up from my cradle age with such care as parents are wont to bestow upon their children whom they mean to make the maintainers of their name . . . They offered learning unto me, especially that kind that breatheth what is truth . . . Neither was I barred from seeing the natural knowledge of things so far as the narrow sight of man hath pierced into it. And because the mind's commandment is vain without the body be enabled to obey it, my strength was exercised with horsemanship, weapons, and such other qualities . . . wherein so I profited that as I was not excellent, so was I accompagnable.[1] After that, by my years or perchance by sooner privilege than years commonly grant, I was thought able to be mine own master, I was suffered to spend some time in travel, that by the comparison of many things I might ripen my judgment . . . Then being home returned and thought of good hope (for the world rarely bestows a better title upon youth) I continued to use the benefits of a quiet mind, in truth (I call Him to witness that knoweth hearts) even in the secret of my soul bent to honesty.

[1] Companionable.

This description of the 'untroubled tenor of a well guided life' corresponds closely with Sidney's earlier career.[1] But suddenly it was disturbed by love, first revealed in a dream of which he gives a long poetic account.

> There came a chariot fair by doves and sparrous
> guided,
> Whose stormlike course stayed not till hard by me
> it bided'
> I, wretch, astonished was, and thought the deathful
> doom
> Of heaven, of earth, of hell, of time and place,
> was come.
> But straight there issued forth two ladies (ladies, sure,
> They seemed to me) on whom did wait a virgin
> pure.

The ladies prove to be the Goddesses Venus and Diana, and the latter addresses the waiting nymph as 'sweet Mira mine',

> To only thee (thou seest) we grant this special grace
> Us to attend in this most private time and place.

Diana then turns to Venus and declares, because of the discord between them, their temples are defaced and their altars lie in the dust. She proposed that there should be perfect peace between them:

> Let one the Princess be, to her the other yield,
> (For vain equality is but contention's field),
> And let her have the gifts that should to both remain,
> In her let beauty both and chasteness fully reign.

As a judge between them she pointed to Philisides, and Venus, mindful of Paris, assented, 'the lad doth please me well'. Each expected to receive the prize of an amber crown, but Philisides bestowed it upon the waiting nymph, Mira. Both Goddesses thereupon cried,

> Fie, fie, what have we done? ungodly rebel, fie!

*       *       *

[1] Brie pointed out that this resembles closely the Seventh Prose in Sannazaro's *Arcadia*. Zandvoort warns against it being taken too closely as autobiographical. It was suppressed in the 1593 folio.

'Yet thou shalt not go free', quoth Venus, 'such a fire
Her beauty kindle shall within thy foolish mind,
That thou full oft shalt wish thy judging eyes were
blind;'
'Nay then', Diana said, 'the chasteness I will give,
In ashes of despair, though burnt, will make thee
live'

The deities thereupon fled to the heavens, and Philisides
awoke, uncertain whether he has merely had a dream.

Was it a dream? O dream, how hast thou wrought in
me,
That I things erst unknown shall first in dreaming
see?

As he continues in prose:

For so indeed it fell out that her I saw, I say that sweet
and incomparable Mira, so like her which in that rather
vision than dream of mine I had seen, that I began to persuade myself in my nativity I was allotted unto her . . .
But having spent some parts of my youth in following her,
sometimes with some measure of favour, sometimes with
unkind interpretations of my most kind thoughts; in the
end having attempted all means to establish my blissful
estate, and having been not only refused of all comfort,
but new quarrels picked against me, I did resolve by per-
petual absence to choke my own evil fortunes.

But before he departed he sent her a farewell in elegiac verse,
which began thus:

Unto a caitiff wretch whom long affliction holdeth,
And now fully believes help to be quite perished,
Grant, yet grant, yet a look to the last monument of
his anguish.
O you (alas so I find) cause of his only ruin,
Dread not a whit (O goodly cruel) that pity may enter
Into thy heart by the sight of this epistle I send.

He compares his present unhappy state with his past bliss:

Shall I not, oh may I not thus yet refresh the
remembrance

What sweet joys I had once, and what a place I
did hold.
Shall I not once object that you, you, granted a favour
Unto the man whom now such miseries you award?
Bend your thoughts to the dear, sweet words which
then to me given were,
Think what a world is now, think who hath altered
her heart.
What, was I then worthy of such good? now worthy
so much evil?
Now fled, then cherished; then so nigh, now so
remote?

Philisides would have gone on telling the rest of his unhappy
adventures, but the shepherd Dicus begged him to forego
for the time being his private grief, and to join in bewailing
the general loss of that country which had become a nurse to
strangers as well as a mother to Arcadians.

Philisides becomes mute and lets Dicus, followed by
another shepherd Agelastus, pour forth long metrical lamentations for Basilius. But posterity would willingly have sacrificed these for further outpourings by Philisides had they
thrown fresh light on the problem of the relation (if any)
between the Philisides – Mira lyrics and the Astrophel-
Stella sonnets. Dobell thought it was sufficiently evident that
the lady here called Mira was the same whom he celebrated
later as Stella. But this seems to me doubtful. The passing
love melancholy of Philisides is very different from the
passionate ardours of Astrophel. And it should be noted that
in the *Arcadia* when Pyrocles falls in love with Philoclea on
seeing her picture, it was because her beauty surpassed that
of the previously beloved Zelmane. Is this a hint of a former
love affair of Sidney, eclipsed by Stella, as Rosaline was for
Romeo by Juliet?

# CHAPTER XXI

## ASTROPHEL AND STELLA –
## EDITIONS – SPONTANEITY – DATE

The *Astrophel and Stella* poems made their first appearance in print five years after Sidney's death, when Thomas Newman issued them in a quarto with a dedicatory letter 'to the worshipful and his very good friend, Mr Francis Flower, Esq.,' wherein he states:

> It was my fortune, not many days ago to light upon the famous device of *Astrophel and Stella*, which carrying the general commendation of all men of judgement, and being reputed to be one of the rarest things that ever any Englishman set abroad, I have thought good to publish it under your name . . . I have been very careful in the printing of it, and whereas being spread abroad in written copies, it had gathered much corruption by ill writers, I have used their help and advice in correcting and restoring it to his first dignity that I know were of skill and experience in such matters.

Did these advisers include Thomas Nashe, who characteristically added 'somewhat to read for them that list'? Nashe begins the lengthy 'somewhat' by bidding the gentlemen, in theatrical imagery,

> that have seen Pan sitting in his bower of delights and a number of Midases to admire his miserable hornpipes, let not your surfeited sights, new come from such puppet play, think scorn to turn aside into this theatre of pleasure, for here you will find a paper stage strewed with pearl, an artificial heaven to overshadow the fair frame, and crystal walls to encounter your curious eyes, whilst the tragicomedy of love is performed by starlight. The chief actor here is Melpomene whose dusky robes dipped in the ink of tears yet seem to drop when I view them near. The argument cruel chastity, the prologue hope, the epilogue despair.

The only consolation for Astrophel's premature loss is that there are still left many goodly branches from the same root of renown, especially the 'fair sister of Phoebus and eloquent secretary to the Muses, most rare Countess of Pembroke . . . whom Arts do adore as a second Minerva, and our poets extol as the patroness of their invention'. This and further flattery of Sidney's sister were doubtless intended as a sop to her justifiable displeasure at the publication of such intimate poems without her consent. And in spite of Newman's claims, the text contained many inaccuracies, some of them absurd.[1] Through the intervention of Burghley the unsold copies were impounded by the Stationers' Company. Yet another publisher, Matthew Lowndes, reprinted Newman's edition with a few corrections and additional mistakes. Before the end of the year, 1591, Newman himself brought out a revised edition, correcting many of the mistakes of his first quarto, and omitting the dedication to Flower, Nashe's 'somewhat' and the sonnets by other hands.

Then seven years elapsed before the authoritative text of *Astrophel and Stella* appeared. It was included in the 1598 folio of Sidney's collected works, published under the sanction of the Countess of Pembroke. Though the readings of Newman's second quarto were mainly retained, there were important emandations and additions. The sonnets were numbered for the first time, and XXXVII with its significant repetition of 'Rich' was added. The songs were placed in their right order among the sonnets, the 8th and the 10th contained additional stanzas, and the 11th was new. Why some other pieces apparently connected with the *Astrophel and Stella* cycle were printed separately among a miscellaneous section of Sidney's poems never before published is a matter for conjecture.

Though some links can be found between Philisides and Astrophel, the general contrast is more striking. The former is dejected because his mistress, Mira, has completely forsaken him. The latter grieves because he has missed the opportunity of winning Stella, though her heart was given

---

[1] The Sonnets were followed by ten Songs 'in variable verse', and by 'sundry other rare Sonnets of divers noblemen and gentlemen', including the Earl of Oxford, Daniel and Campion.

to him. And correspondingly significant is the difference of
expression of their woes. Nothing could be more traditionally
fanciful than the dream in which Philisides gives the preference to Mira over the two conflicting Olympian Goddesses,
only to be later rejected by her. On the other hand, Astrophel
from the outset, in sonnet I, stresses that all that he writes is
spontaneous and not derivative.

> Loving in truth, and fair my love in verse to show,
> That the dear She might take some pleasure of my
> > pain.
> Pleasure might cause her read, reading might make
> > her know,
> Knowledge might pity win, and pity grace obtain,
> I sought fit words to paint the blackest face of woe,
> Studying inventions fine her wits to entertain,
> Oft turning others' leaves to see if thence would flow
> Some fresh and fruitful shower upon my sun-burnt
> > brain
> But words came halting out, wanting invention's stay.
> Invention, Nature's child, fled stepdame's Study's
> > blows
> And others' feet still seemed but strayers in my way.
> Thus, great with child to speak and helpless in my
> > throes,
> Biting my truant pen,[1] beating myself for spite,
> 'Fool', said my Muse to me, 'look in thy heart and
> > write.'

It should be noted that Sidney uses the word 'invention' here
in almost the opposite of its customary modern meaning; it
is akin to its Wordsworthian sense of the faculty that pierces
to the essential realities, in this case of emotion. Again and
again, with the most earnest imagery, he makes claim to
poetic originality.

In III he is not one of

> Pindar's apes, flaunt they in phrases fine,
> Enam'ling with pied flowers their thoughts of gold.

---

[1] Newman's first quarto of 1591 has 'my tongue and pen'.

Nor is he a Euphuist, one of those who

> With strange similes enrich each line
> Of herbs or beasts which Ind or Afrie hold.

Nor does he have recourse to paradoxical antitheses (VI).

> Some lovers speak, when they their Muses entertain,
> Of hopes begot by fear, of wot not what desires; –
> Of force of heavenly beams infusing hellish fires;
> Of living deaths, dear wounds, fair storms, and
> freezing fires.

There are others who ransack mythology and allegorize their emotions in stories of Leda, Europa and Danäe:

> Some one his song in Jove and Jove's strange tales
> attires,
> Bordered with bulls and swans, powdered with golden
> rain.

Others again adopt a pastoral disguise.

> Another humbler wit to shepherd's pipe retires,
> Yet hiding royal blood full oft in rural vein.

This is a curious indictment for Sidney to make for it describes the stratagem adopted by his own Musidorus in *Arcadia*. In XV he makes a more comprehensive arraignment. There are those who seek to revive faded flowers of rhetoric from old Parnassus. Others pray in aid alliteration:

> Ye that do dictionary's method bring
> Into your rhymes, running in rattling rows.

Some blow on the ashes of a dead romance, and

> Poor Petrarch's long deceased woes
> With new-born sighs and denisen'd[1] wit do sing.

All have gone astray.

> You take wrong ways: those far-fet helps be such
> As do betray a want of inward touch,
> And sure at length stolen goods do come to light.

With all these he contrasts himself later in LXXIV.

---

[1] Enfranchised, naturalized.

I never drank of Aganippe well
Nor ever did in shade of Tempe sit.

\* \* \*

And this I swear by blackest brook of Hell,
I am no pick-purse of another's art.
How falls it, then, that with so smooth an ease
My thoughts I speak? and what I speak I show
In verse, and that my verse best wits doth please?
Guess we the cause? What, is it thus? Fie, no.
Or so? Much less. How then? Sure thus it is,
My lips are sweet, inspired by Stella's kiss.

Yet it was impossible for Sidney, as it was for Shakespeare, to stand entirely aloof from the Renaissance poetic tradition. Had not Petrarch poured forth his long deceased woes in a sonnet sequence Sidney would not have used this particular instrument. And had not Surrey employed the English form of the sonnet with its three alternate rhymed quatrains and final couplet, Sidney would probably not have mingled this with the Petrarchan form, though he often makes an effective technical variation by using only two rhymes instead of four in the octave. Indeed throughout the dexterity of his handling of the different rhyme-schemes is remarkable, though he works in accepted moulds.

Modern research has even revealed close parallels between a few of Sidney's sonnets and contemporary French or Latin poems. Take the allusive XXV:

The wisest scholar of the wight most wise,
By Phoebus' doom with sugared sentence sought
That virtue, if it once met with our eyes,
Strange flames of love it in our souls would raise.

\* \* \*

Virtue of late with virtuous care to stir
Love of herself, took Stella's shape that she
To mortal eyes might sweetly shine in her.

The adroit turn thus given to the doctrines of Plato, the scholar of Socrates, in the *Phaedrus* had been anticipated (as Miss Janet Scott has pointed out)[1] by Marc-Claude de

---

[1] *Les sonnets élizabéthains: les sources et l'apport personnel*, p. 43.

Buttet in his *L'Amalthée*, published at Lyons in 1575.

> Si la vertu, divinèment connue
> De l'esprit seul, à l'oeil se faisait voir,
> (Comme tu as, grand Platon, fait scavoir)
> De quel amour seroit nostre ame émue.

For him Virtue has become visibly embodied in his beloved.

> La Vertue seule adorée de moi.

The parallel is so close that it can scarcely be accidental. And take again XVII with its exquisite picture of Cupid weeping because his mother Venus has broken his bow and shafts,

> Till that his grandame, Nature, pitying it,
> Of Stella's brows made him two better bows,
> And in her eyes of arrows infinite

Miss Scott has unearthed a Latin poem by the fifteenth-century humanist, Pontanus, whose beloved, like Sidney's, was called Stella, which contains a similar picture of Cupid being comforted for the loss of his bow and arrows.

> Neve, puer, neu fle, mater! dant spicula mille
> Stellae oculi; puer, his autere pro pharetra.

Even if more of such parallels were to be discovered, they would not invalidate Sidney's proud claim for the spontaneity of his Muse in *Astrophel and Stella* as a whole. Unlike *Philisides and Mira*, as it seems to me, this cycle was born of a passionately felt personal experience, though it partook, especially in its earlier phases, of features reminiscent of *The Defence of Poesie*. With its first publication in 1591 and its final revision in 1598, the dates of its composition are doubtful. But two sonnets can be dated with sufficient certainty. In XXX Sidney avows that his preoccupation as a lover prevents him from giving anything but superficial answers to those who question him on international problems.

> Whether the Turkish new-moon minded be
> To fill his horns this year on Christian coast?
> How Poles' right King means without leave of host.
> To warm with ill-made fire cold Muscovy?
> If French can yet three parts in one agree?

What now the Dutch in their full diets boast?
How Holland hearts, now so good towns be lost,
Trust in the shade of pleasing Orange-tree.
How Ulster likes of that same golden bit
Wherewith my father once made it half tame?
If in the Scotch Court be no weltring yet?

A. W. Pollard in his edition of *Astrophel and Stella* gives the probable explanation of these allusions, and showed that they fitted in best with the early period of 1581. Incidentally it may be noted that merely in enumerating these complex foreign issues Sidney, in spite of his disclaimer, shows himself to be a constant political observer. In the other dating sonnet, XLI, he appears as the gallant courtier and man-at-arms.

Having this day my horse, my hand, my lance
Guided so well that I obtain'd the prize,
Both by the judgement of the English eyes,
And of some sent from that sweet enemy France.

Various onlookers praised him for various reasons.

How far they shot awry! the true cause is
Stella looked on, and from her heavenly face
Sent forth the beams which made so fair my race.

The tourney in which Sidney was victor was one of those which took place while French envoys, on behalf of Elizabeth's marriage with the Duke of Anjou, were over in England between April and August 1581.

This period was also momentous in Sidney's personal relations. It will be remembered that the Earl of Essex had been anxious for a match between his daughter, Penelope Devereux, and Philip. But the Earl had died in September 1576, and two years later Sidney's uncle, the Earl of Leicester, to whom he was expectant heir, had married the widowed Countess. When a child was born to them, Sidney's prospects were completely altered. It was probably on this account that Penelope's relatives hurried her in the spring of 1581, when she was between eighteen and nineteen, into marriage with the wealthy Lord Rich, who had recently succeeded to his father's title and estates. The significant play upon his name in XXIV puts it beyond doubt that it is he whom Sidney has in mind.

> Rich fools there be . . . [who] more rich, more
>                                       wretched grow.
> Yet to those fools Heaven doth such wit impart
> As what their hands do hold, their heads do know,
> And knowing, love; and loving lay apart
> As sacred things, far from all danger's show.
> But that rich fool, who by blind Fortune's lot
> The richest gem of love and life enjoys,
> And can with foul abuse such beauties blot,
> Let him, depriv'd of sweet but unfelt joys,
> Exil'd for aye from those high treasures, which
> He knows not, grow in only folly rich.

Pollard held that all the first thirty sonnets except this were written before Penelope's marriage, and his view has found acceptance. But have we the right arbitrarily to exclude this one sonnet which goes against this theory, and which keeps its place unchanged through the successive editions? Is it not safer to assume that the whole group were written after Penelope's marriage? In any case XXIV is closely linked with XXXVII, which made its first appearance in the 1598 folio, and where the provocative name of his supplanter stirs him to play upon it with even more mordant reiteration.

> Towards Aurora's Court a nymph doth dwell,
> Rich in all beauties which man's eye can see.
> Beauties so far from reach of words that we
> Abuse her praise, saying she doth excel:
> Rich in the measure of deserv'd renown,
> Rich in the riches of a royal heart.
> Rich in those gifts which give th' eternal crown:
> Which, though most rich in these and every part
> Which make the patents of true worldly bliss,
> Hath no misfortune, but that Rich she is.

The catastrophic paradox of the last line is accentuated by the capitalization of Rich, here no longer an epithet but a proper name. Now that Penelope, his star, his Stella, is another's he deplores the opportunity he has missed.

# CHAPTER XXII

# 'ASTROPHEL AND STELLA' – SONGS – JOY AND DISILLUSION

He admits in sonnet II, which is a prologue to the cycle, that his passion had been of only gradual growth.

> Not at the first sight, nor with a dribléd[1] shot
> Love gave the wound which, while I breathe, will
> bleed.
> But known worth did in mine of time proceed,
> Till by degrees it had full conquest got.
> I saw and liked: I liked but lovéd not.
> I loved, but straight did not what love decreed.
> At length to Love's decrees I forc'd, agreed,
> Yet with repining at so partial lot.
> Now even that footstep of lost liberty
> Is gone, and now like slave-born Muscovite,
> I call it peace to suffer tyranny;
> And now employ the remnant of my wit
> To make myself believe that all is well,
> While, with a feeling skill, I paint my hell.

The last sombre phrase is echoed in the opening quatrian of XXXIII.

> I might! – unhappy word – O me, I might,
> And then would not, or could not see my bliss,
> Till now wrapt in a most infernal night,
> I find how heavenly day, wretch, I did miss.
> Heart, rent thyself, thou dost thyself but right:
> No lovely Paris made thy Helen his;
> No force, no fraud robbed thee of thy delight,
> Nor Fortune of thy fortune author was,
> But to myself myself did give the blow.

In lines that have in themselves a somnolent rhythm he seeks refuge from his anguish in sleep (XXXIX).

[1] Slowly sped.

Come, sleep! O sleep, the certain knot of peace,
The baiting place of wit, the balm of woe;
The poor man's wealth, the prisoner's release,
The indifferent judge between the high and low:
With shield of proof shield me from out the press
Of those fierce darts despair at me doth throw.
O make in me those civil wars to cease.
I will good tribute pay, if thou do so,
Take thou of me smooth pillows, sweetest bed,
A chamber deaf to noise, and blind to sight.

For a time his lamentations are fruitless (XLIV).

My words, I know, do well set forth my mind,
My mind bemoans his sense of inward smart:
Such smart may pity claim of any heart.
Her heart, sweet heart, is of no tiger's kind:
And yet she hears, and yet no pity I find;
The more I cry, less grace she doth impart.

Or again (XLV):

Stella oft sees the very face of woe
Painted in my beclouded, stormy face,
But cannot skill to pity my disgrace,
Not though the cause thereof *herself* she know.

Yet lately the fictitious tale of two lovers' grievous case drew
tears in pity from her eyes. Let her then see in him such an
imaginary martyr.

Then think, my dear, that you in me do read
Of lovers' ruin some sad tragedy.
And if not me, pity the tale of me.

He seeks again to shake off her spell (XLVII).

Virtue, awake! Beauty but beauty is:
I may, I must, I can, I will, I do
Leave following that which it is gain to miss.
Let her go! Soft, but here she comes! Go to!
Unkind, I love you not. O me, that eye
Doth make my heart give to my tongue the lie.

Here at any rate, if the words are to be taken literally, she admits him to her presence, though with a paradoxical result in LX.

> When my good angel guides me to the place
> Where all my good I do in Stella see,
> That heav'n of joys throws only down on me
> Thundered disdains and lightnings of disgrace.
> But when the rugged'st step of Fortune's race,
> Makes me fall from her sight, then sweetly she,
> With words wherin the Muses' treasures be,
> Shows love and pity on my absent case.
> Now I, wit-beaten long by hardest fate,
> So dull am that I cannot look into
> The ground of this fierce love and lovely hate.
> Then, some good body, tell me how I do,
> Whose presence absence, absence presence is,
> Blissed in my curse, and cursèd in my bliss.

When Sidney wrote those last four lines he seems to have forgotten how in sonnet VI he had mocked at the lovers who speak in their poems,

> Of living deaths, dear wounds, fair storms and
>                                         freezing fires.

But his agitated words point to a softening of Stella's attitude towards him, and in the next sonnet we hear her 'sweet breath'd defence' to his importunity:

> That who indeed infelt affection bears
> So captives to his Saint both soul and sense
> That, wholly *hers*, all selfness he forbears:
> Thence his desires he learns, his life's course thence.
> Now since her chaste mind hates this love in me
> With chastened mind I straight must show that she
> Shall quickly me from what she hates remove.

Knowing the intensity of his own passion he asks Doctor Cupid to reply for him,

> Driv'n else to grant, by angel's sophistry,
> That I love not without I leave to love.

Even more explicit is LXII:

> Late tir'd with woe, even ready for to pine
> With rage of love, I call'd my love unkind;
> She in whose eyes love, though unfelt, doth shine,
> Sweet said that I true love in her should find.
> I joyed, but straight thus watered was my wine,
> That love she did, but loved a love not blind,
> Which would not let me, whom she loved, decline
> From nobler course, fit for my birth and mind:
> And therefore by her love's authority
> Willed me these tempests of vain love to fly,
> And anchor fast myself on Virtue's shore.

Sidney now can summon up enough courage to reply direct:

> Alas, if this the only metal be
> Of love new-coined to help my beggary,
> Dear, love me not, that you may love me more.

He can even playfully find comfort in her 'No, No!' to his request for the thing which ever she denies (LXIII).

> Sing then, my Muse, now 'Io Paean' sing!
> Heav'n envy not at my high triumphing,
> But grammar's force with sweet success confirm,
> For grammar says – O this, dear Stella, say –
> For grammar says – (to grammar who says nay?)
> That in one speech two negatives affirm.

With dialogue and with verbal *tour-de-forces* Sidney in this group of sonnets has strained their narrow bounds to the utmost, and he may have found technical relief in turning to the lyrical rhythm of the first of his songs.

> Doubt you to whom my Muse these notes intendeth,
> Which now my breast, o'ercharged to music lendeth.
> To *you*, to *you*, all song of praise is due:
> Only to *you* my song begins and endeth.

This is literally true for the last verse repeats the first, and in those between which pay tribute to Stella's different attractions there is no variation in the third line. The climax is in the penultimate verse.

Who hath the voice which soul from senses sunders?
Whose force but yours the bolts of beauty thunders?
To *you*, to *you*, all song of praise is due:
Only with *you* no miracles are wonders.

In sonnets LXVI and LXVII there is the rising note of hope, which finds its exultant realization in LXIX.

O joy too high for my low style to show!
O bliss fit for a nobler state than me.

\*　　\*　　\*

Gone is the winter of my misery.
My Spring appears. O see what here doth grow,
For Stella hath, with words where faith doth shine,
Of her high heart given me the monarchy.
I, I, O, I, may say that she is mine!
And though she give but thus conditionally,
This realm of bliss, while virtuous course I take,
No Kings be crown'd but they some covenants make.

But Sidney's acquiescence in this limited monarchy is short-lived. In the second song he tells how he steals a kiss from Stella's lips while she is asleep. Then follow other kisses, when she is awake, but on condition that he keeps them secret (LXXXI).

O kiss, which souls, even souls, together ties
By links of love, and only Nature's art,
How fain would I paint thee to all men's eyes,
Or of thy gifts at least set out some part.
But she forbids: with blushing words she says
She builds her fame on higher seated praise.
But my heart burns; I cannot silent be.

This is fortunate for us, as otherwise we might have forfeited the exquisite group of songs in which Sidney pours forth his passion and has Stella's answer. In the fourth song it is a night-time meeting.

Night hath closed all in her cloak;
Twinkling stars love-thoughts provoke.
Danger hence good care doth keep,
Jealousy itself doth sleep.

> Take me to thee, and thee to me.
> 'No, no, no, no, my dear, let be.'

If Sidney could pretend that two 'no's' made an affirmative he could not extend this fancy to four. But one stanza in this song seems out of place.

> Your fair mother is abed,
> Candles out and curtains spread.
> She thinks you do letters write;
> Write, but let me first endite,
> 'Take me to thee, and thee to me.'
> 'No, no, no, no, my dear, let be.'

If Sidney was here pleading to Lady Rich, one would have thought that not her mother but her husband would have been her guardian. It has to be assumed that, in Miss Mona Wilson's words, 'he rides down to see her mother's house in the country, believing that at last she will surrender'. Our knowledge of Lord Rich is fragmentary, and Sidney's invective against him in the role of the jealous husband may have to be in part discounted (LXXVIII).

> Who since he hath by Nature's special grace,
> So piercing jaws as spoil when they embrace,
> So nimble feet as stir still, though on thorns,
> So many eyes, aye seeking their own woe;
> So ample ears as never good news know:
> Is it not evil, that such a devil wants horns?

But Sidney cannot count upon Stella's continued favour (LXXXVI).

> Alas! whence came this change of looks? If I
> Have chang'd desert, let mine own conscience be
> A still-felt plague to self condemning me.
> Let woe grip on my heart, shame load mine eye.
> But if all faith, like spotless ermine, be
> Safe in my soul, which only doth to thee,
> As his sole object of felicity,
> With wings of love in air of wonder fly,
> O ease your hand, treat not so hard your slave;
> In justice pains come not till faults do call.

At last her changed attitude provokes him into rebellion in the fifth song.

> While favour fed my hope, delight with hope was
> brought;
> Thought waited on delight, and speech did follow
> thought;
> Then drew my tongue and pen records unto thy glory.
>
> \*     \*     \*
>
> I said thou wert most fair, and so indeed thou art;
> I said thou wert most sweet, sweet poison to my heart;
> I said my soul was thine – O that I then had lied!
> I said thine eyes were stars, thy breast the milken way,
> Thy fingers Cupid's shafts, thy voice the angels' lay;
> And all I said so well as no man it denied.

But now that he has lost hope,

> I think now of thy faults, who late thought of thy
> praise;
> That speech falls now to blame which did thy
> honour raise.

He calls upon his Muse to come to the aid of 'your client, poor myself':

> Revenge! revenge! my Muse! Defiance trumpet blow,
> Threat'n what may be done, yet do more than you
> threat'n.

He terms her in mounting succession thief, murdering tyrant, witch, devil – only to end,

> Alas! yet still of me beloved.
> You see what I can say. Mend yet your froward mind,
> And such skill in my Muse you, reconcil'd, shall find.
> That all these cruel words your praises shall be proved.

In the eighth song, perfect in its fusion of lyric and dramatic strains, the decisive point is reached.

> In a grove most rich of shade,
> Where birds wanton music made,

Astrophel with Stella sweet
Did for mutual comfort meet,
Both within themselves oppressèd,
But each in the other blessèd!

Love moves Astrophel to make his urgent plea.

'Stella, sovereign of my joy,
Fair triumpher of annoy;
Stella, star of heavenly fire,
Stella, lodestar of desire:

\*      \*      \*

Stella, whose voice, when it speaks,
Senses all asunder breaks;
Stella, whose voice, when it singeth,
Angels to acquaintance bringeth:

Grant – O dear, on knees I pray,
(Knees on ground he then did stay)
'That, not I, but since I love you,
Time and place for me may move you.

Never season was more fit,
Never room more apt for it;
Smiling air allows my reason;
These birds sing, "Now use the season".

This small wind, which so sweet is,
See how it the leaves doth kiss;
Each tree in his best attiring
Sense of love to love inspiring.

Love makes earth the water drink,
Love to earth makes water sink;
And, if dumb things be so witty,
Shall a heavenly grace want pity?'

Having thus set forth precedents for his love-making even
from inanimate nature, Astrophel sought to make his hands
too speak for him, but Stella repelled them.

'Astrophel,' said she, 'my love,
Cease in these effects to prove;
Now be still, yet still believe me,
Thy grief more than death would grieve me.

If that any thought in me
Can taste comfort but of thee,
Let me, fed with hellish anguish,
Joyless, hopeless, endless languish.

    *    *    *

If more may be said, I say,
All my bliss in thee I lay;
If thou love, my love content thee,
For all love, all faith is meant thee.

Trust me, while I thee deny
In myself the smart I try;
Tyrant honour doth thus use thee,
Stella's self might not refuse thee.

Therefore, dear, this no more move,
Lest, though I leave not thy love,
Which too deep in me is framéd
I should blush when thou art naméd.'

Therewithal away she went,
Leaving him to passion rent
With what she had done and spoken,
That therewith my song is broken.

Stella here, as Sidney puts it, in sonnet LXXXVII, takes her
stand upon the laws of duty! She gives her heart to Astrophel
but only so long as he remains a stainless Sir Galahad. Never
has conscience triumphant over sensual desire found more
arresting utterance than in the accents that fall from her lips.
They are an Elizabethan *Ode to Duty*,

A light to guide, a rod
To check the erring, and reprove.

Virtue and passion look each other in the face, and part.

It is something of an anti-climax that in the ninth song Sidney for the first time in this cycle turns to pastoral imagery.

> Go, my flock, go, get you hence,
> Seek a better place of feeding
>
> \*　　\*　　\*
>
> Stella hath refusèd me,
> Stella, who more love hath provèd
> In this caitiff heart to be
> Than can in good ewes be movèd
> Toward lambkins best belovèd.
>
> \*　　\*　　\*
>
> Why, alas, doth she then swear
> That she loveth me so dearly?
>
> \*　　\*　　\*
>
> No, she hates me (welaway!)
> Feigning love, somewhat to please me,
> Knowing if she should display
> All her hate, death soon would seize me,
> And of hideous torments ease me.

But this is a passing mood, and though he tries to make the best of 'Absence' from his 'dear Captain', his eager questioning of one who has seen her reveals how she fills his thoughts (XCII).

> When I demand of Phoenix Stella's state,
> You say, forsooth, you left her well of late.
> O God! think you that satisfies my care?
> I would know whether she did sit or walk,
> How cloth'd; how waited on; sighed she or smiled?
> Whereof, with whom, how often did she talk?
> With what pastime time's journey she beguiled?
> If her lips deigned to sweeten my poor name?
> Say all; and all well said, still say the same.

In a tenth song he bids his 'thought' represent him with Stella, and every stanza begins with 'thought' or 'think'.

Thought, therefore, I will send thee
To take up the place for me;
Long I will not often tarry:
There, unseen, thou mayest be bold
Those fair wonders to behold,
Which in them my hopes do carry.

\*       \*       \*

Think, think, of those dallyings,
When with dove-like murmurings,
With glad moaning, passed anguish
We change eyes and heart for heart
Each to other do depart,
Joying till joy makes us languish.

\*       \*       \*

O my thought, my thoughts surcease;
Thy delights my woes increase
My life melts with too much thinking:
Think no more, but die in me
Till thou shalt revivèd be,
At her lips my nectar drinking.

Nearly all that follows is in a lower key. In XCIII he asks,
'What ink is black enough to paint my woe?' because he has
vexed her. His thought welcomes night (XCVI) because
they both wear the same black livery. 'Night barred from
sun, thou from thy own sunlight.' Yet bed, which invites
him to steal some rest (XCVIII), is but a field wherein to
turn and toss. Stella also lies on a sick bed (CI), but is soon
well enough to be borne on the 'happy Thames', when 'the
boat for joy could not to dance forbear' (CIII). And she even
in the eleventh song can give ear for a time to her lover's
serenade, though there is no longer the tenderness on her
lips as when they met in a grove most rich of shade.

"Who is it that this dark night
Underneath my window plaineth?"
'It is one who from thy sight
Being, ah, exiled, disdaineth
Every other vulgar light.'

"Why, alas, and are you he?
Be not yet those fancies changèd?"
'Dear, when you find change in me
Though from me you be estrangèd,
Let my change to ruin be.'

\*        \*        \*

"But time will these thoughts remove:
Time doth work what no man knoweth."
'Time doth as the subject prove;
With time still the affection groweth
In the faithful turtle dove.'

"What if you new beauties see
Will not they stir new affection?"
'I will think they pictures be,
(Image like of saints' perfection)
Poorly counterfeiting thee.'

\*        \*        \*

"Peace! I think that some gives ear
Come no more, lest I get anger."
'Bliss, I will my bliss forbear,
Fearing, sweet, you to endanger;
But my soul shall harbour there.'

"Well, be gone! be gone, I say;
Lest that Argus' eyes perceive you."
'O unjust fortune's sway
Which can make me thus to leave you,
And from louts to run away.'

Yet he had been misled into counting on another meeting
(CVI).

O absent presence! Stella is not here!
False, flattering hope, that with so fair a face
Bare me in hand, that in this orphan place
Stella, I say, my Stella, should appear.

And in the last sonnet (CVIII) the thought of her brings
mingled joy and woe:

But soon as thought of thee breeds my delight,
And my young soul flutters to thee, his nest,
Most rude despair, my daily unbidden guest,
Clips straight my wings, straight wraps me in his night,
And makes me then bow down my head and say,
'Ah, what doth Phoebus' gold that wretch avail
Whom iron doors do keep from use of day?'
So strangely, alas, thy works in me prevail
That in my woes for thee thou art my joy,
And in my joys for thee my only annoy.

Such was the close of *Astrophel and Stella* in the 1598 folio under the direction of the Countess of Pembroke. Presumably she had some warrant for not including in the cycle, but in a miscellaneous section never before printed, some pieces apparently suitable to the major sequence, and of equal poetic quality. Among these may be singled out another of Sidney's captivating songs.

Ring out your bells, let mourning shows be spread,
For Love is dead:
All Love is dead, infected
With plague of deep disdain:
Worth, as nought worth rejected,
And Faith fair scorn doth gain.
From so ungrateful fancy,
From such a female franzy;
From them that use men thus,
Good Lord, deliver us!

*       *       *

Let dirge be sung, and Trentals rightly read,
For Love is dead.
Sir Wrong his tomb ordaineth:
My mistress marble-heart,
Which epitaph containeth
 Her eyes were once his dart.'
From so ungrateful fancy,
From such a female franzy;
From them that use men thus,
Good Lord, deliver us!

Alas! I lie: rage hath this error bred;
Love is not dead:
Love is not dead, but sleepeth
In her unmatchèd mind,
Where she his counsel keepeth
Till due desert she find
Therefore from so vile fancy,
To call such wit a franzy,
Who Love can temper thus,
Good Lord, deliver us!

But the Countess was better advised than the modern
editor, A. B. Grosart, who placed the last two of the previously unprinted sonnets, with their 'posy' at the end of
*Astrophel and Stella*. In the former of these he takes leave of
his sensual promptings:

Desire! Desire! I have too clearly bought
With prize of mangled mind thy worthless ware.
Too long, too long, asleep thou hast me brought
Who should my mind to higher things prepare!

And in its sequel he has bent himself to that aim:

Leave me, O Love, which reachest but to dust,
And thou, my mind, aspire to higher things:
Grow rich in that which never taketh rust;
What ever fades but fading pleasure brings.
Draw in thy beams, and humble all thy might
To that sweet yoke where lasting freedoms be
Which breaks the clouds, and opens forth the light,

That doth both shine, and give us sight to see.
O take fast hold; let that light be thy guide
In the small course which birth draws out to death,
And think how evil becometh him to slide
Who seeketh heav'n, and comes of heav'nly breath.
Then farewell world; thy uttermost I see:
Eternal Love, maintain thy life in me!
*Splendidis longum valedico nugis.*

It is a saintly valediction but one not fitting to the lips of
Astrophel. Though in his love for Stella there has been

throughout the stirring of the senses that is termed 'desire', it is fused with a super-sensual idealism of Platonic origin, for which no apology was needed. It should be remembered that a similar bond linked Pyrocles to Philoclea in the *Arcadia*. While therefore the *Astrophel and Stella* cycle has its basis in the true and moving story of Philip Sidney and Penelope Devereux, it probably admitted an element of dramatic fantasy. This would go some way to solve the double paradox with which we are otherwise left. Stella gives her heart to Astrophel but keeps her marriage vows. Penelope is unfaithful to Lord Rich with Charles Blount (afterwards Lord Mountjoy), to whom she had been secretly betrothed, and whom, after her divorce, she married. Astrophel is to the end constant to Stella, his only light, of whom all other beauties are poor counterfeits. Sidney before very long was to find a wife in Frances, the daughter of Sir Francis Walsingham. Here are riddles which provide headaches for a biographer who is not satisfied by terming Penelope a minx or flirt, and seeing in Sidney's courtship of Frances the reaction after a fruitless grand passion. But for the lover of poetry there is more than ample compensation. Into the orbit of this passion there is nothing too high or too low, from the moon to a lapdog and a sparrow, from Greek philosophy to grammar rules, that Sidney cannot invoke. Even when lovelorn he can display the catholicity of outlook which I have sought to illustrate from the *Arcadia*.

# CHAPTER XXIII

# TRANSLATIONS – THE PSALMS – 'TREWNESS OF THE CHRISTIAN RELIGION'

In addition to his experiments in original verse, Sidney devoted considerable time and pains to translation. Of this the most important outcome was his version of forty-three of the Psalms from the Vulgate. This is preserved, together with the translation by the Countess of Pembroke of the others, in a number of manuscripts of which the chief are Rawlinson 25 in the Bodleian, transcribed by Samuel Woodford, and the Davies MS. in the Sidney Papers. In 1877 Grosart printed Sidney's part of the translation from the Rawlinson MS. and in 1923 Feuillerat, more accurately, from the Davies.

The value of Sidney's translation of the Psalms has, in my opinion, been underrated by most modern commentators. If compared with the rendering in the Book of Common Prayer it will be found, especially if judged by Elizabethan standards, sufficiently close to the original. But its main attraction lies in its metrical virtuosity. Sidney constantly varies his stanzaic forms, and shows special skill in his manipulation of dissyllabic rhymes, in which English is not abundant. It is not possible to quote here complete psalms, but some illustrative verses may be given.

From Psalm III, stanzas 1 and 2.

Lord, how do they increase
That hatefull never cease
    To breed my grievous trouble.
How many ones there be
That all against poor me
    Their numbrous strength redouble.

Even multitudes be they
That to my soul do say
'No help for you remaineth

In God on whom you build,'
Yet, Lord, thou art my shield,
In thee my glory reigneth.'

From Psalm VI, stanzas 2 and 3.

But mercy, Lord, let mercy thine descend,
For I am weak, and in my weakness languish.
Lord, help, for ev'n my bones their marrow spend
With cruel anguish.

Nay ev'n my soul fell troubles do appal!
Alas, how long my God wilt thou delay me?
Turn thee, sweet Lord, and from this ugly fall
My dear God, stay me.

Here Sidney has added emphasis to the Biblical appeals.
From Psalm XIX, stanzas 1 and 2.

The heav'nly frame sets forth the fame
Of him that only thunders;
The firmament so strangely bent
Shows his hand-working wonders.

Day unto day it doth display,
Their course doth it acknowledge;
And night to night succeeding right
In darkness teach clear knowledge.

As if in proof of his versatility Sidney throughout this psalm
of sixteen stanzas maintains, in addition to the dissyllabic
rhyme in lines 2 and 4, an internal rhyme in lines 1 and 3.
The short Psalm XXIII with its pastoral imagery would
make a special appeal to the author of the *Arcaida*, and may
be exceptionally reproduced in full.

The Lord, the Lord, my shepherd is,
And so can never I
Taste misery,
He rests me in green pasture his:
By waters still and sweet
He guides my feet.

He me revives, leads me the way
　　Which righteousness doth take
　　　　For his name's sake.
Yea, though I should through valleys stray
　　Of death's dark shade, I will
　　　　No whit fear ill.

For thou, dear Lord, thou me beset'st:
　　Thy rod and thy staff be
　　　　To comfort me:
Before me thou a table set'st
　　Even when foes' envious eye
　　　　Doth it espy.

Thou oil'st my head, thou fill'st my cup,
　　Nay more thine endless good
　　　　Shalt give me food.
To thee, I say, ascended up
　　Where thou the Lord of all
　　　　Dost hold thy hall.

In contrast with the above are the resonant closing stanzas
of Psalm XXIV.

Lift up your heads, you gates; and you doors ever
　　　　　　　　　　　　　　　　　biding.
　　In comes the King of glory bright.
Who is this glorious King, in might and power riding?
　　The Lord whose strength makes battles fight.

Lift up your heads, you gates, and you doors ever
　　　　　　　　　　　　　　　　　biding.
　　In comes the King of glory bright.
Who is this glorious King, the lord of armies guiding?
　　Even he the King of glory hight.

An interesting metrical variant appears in Psalm XXX,
which is in *terza rima*, as in stanzas 4 to 7.

Praise, praise the Lord then evermore,
Ye saints of his, remembering still
With thanks his holiness therefore.

For quickly ends his wrathful will;
But his dear favour where it lies
From age to age life joys doth fall.

Well may the evening clothe the eyes
In clouds of tears, but soon as sun
Doth rise again, new joys shall rise.

For proof, while I my race did run
Full of success, fond[1] I did say
That I should never be undone.

In Psalm XXXIII the short-lined stanzas, as the first three
will show, catch faithfully the note of rejoicing:

Rejoice in God, O ye
That righteous be;
For cheerful thankfulness
It is a comely part
In them, whose heart
Doth cherish rightfulness.

O praise with heart the Lord!
O now accord
Viols with singing voice!
Let ten-string'd instrument
O now be bent,
To witness you rejoice.

A new, sing a new song
To him most strong,
Sing loud and merrily,
Because that word of his
Most righteous is,
And his deeds faithful be.

And almost before breaking off from his task of translation
in Psalm XLII, the mingled emotions were expressed by
Sidney in eight-lined stanzas with the unusual feature of a
couple of dissyllabic rhymes, illustrated in the first two
stanzas and the last.

[1] Foolish

As the chafed hart which brayeth,
Seeking some refreshing brook,
To my soul in panting playeth,
Thirsting on my God to look.
    My soul thirsts indeed in me
After ever-loving thee.
Ah, when comes my blessed being,
Of thy face to have a seeing?

Day and night my tears out-flowing
Have been my ill feeding food:
With their daily questions throwing,
'Where is now thy God so good?'
    My heart melts remembr'ing so
How in troops I wont to go,
Leading them, his praises singing,
Holy dance to God's house bringing.
        *        *        *
Why art thou, my soul, so sorry,
And in me so much dismayed?
Wait on God, for yet his glory
In my song shall be displayed;
    To him my thanks shall be said,
Who is still my present aid;
And in fine my soul be raisèd
God is my God, by me praisèd.

It was in much of the same devotional spirit in which he
rendered forty-three Psalms into English that Sidney began
the translation of a prose treatise by his Huguenot friend,
Philip Du Plessis Mornay, *De la Verité de la Religion Chré-
tienne*. Sidney had put into English the length 'Preface to
the Reader' and the first six chapters when he had to leave
for military service in the Netherlands, and entrusted the
rest of the undertaking to Arthur Golding, the translator of
Ovid's *Metamorphoses*. The composite book was published
by Thomas Cadman soon after Sidney's death in 1587 under
the title of *A Work concerning the Trewness of the Christian
Religion*, and dedicated to the Earl of Leicester. Golding,
beyond saying that Sidney 'had proceeded certain chapters

therein', gave no indication of where the division between the two translators began. But Professor Feuillerat in Volume III of his Cambridge edition of Sidney's *Works* solved the problem on the internal evidence of style. Golding, as in his other known translations, aims at literal accuracy, and renders the French word for word. Sidney, on the other hand, while completely accurate, gives to the discourse an additional lucidity and beauty. 'One might very well suppose', states Feuillerat, 'that the book was originally written in English.' And I would add that the style has nothing of the rhetorical elegance of the higher flights in the later *Arcadia*. Here is a specimen extract from the first chapter on the consent of all nations to the existence of God.

> Let a man run from East to West, and from South to North: let him ransack all ages one after another: and wheresoever he findeth any men, there shall he find also a kind of religion and serving of God, with prayers and sacrifices. The diversity whereof is very great, but yet they have always consented all in this point, that there is a God. And as touching the diversity which is in that behalf, it beareth witness that it is a doctrine not delivered closely from people to people, but also bred and brought up with every of them in their own climate, yea and even in their own selves. Within these hundred years many nations have been discovered, and many are daily discovered still, which were unknown in former ages. Among them some have been found to live without Law, without King, without house, going stark naked and wandering abroad in the fields, but yet none without some knowledge of God, none without some spice of Religion: to show unto us that it is not so natural a thing in man to love company, and to clad himself against hurts of the weather (which things we esteem to be very kindly) as it is natural unto him to know the author of his life, that is to say, God.

In this passage Sidney would be interested not only in the central argument but in the reference to the contemporary discovery of new nations which would appeal to his zeal for exploration. In succeeding chapters he was doubtless strongly attracted by another Renaissance feature of Du Plessis Mornay's discourse, the reliance upon the testimony of Greek and Roman authors to one only God.

Among the ancient philosophers, Aristotle appears to have held the first place in Sidney's estimation, and a reference by John Hoskyns in his *Figures of Rhetoric* is of special interest. He states that Sidney had shown his knowledge of Aristotle's *Rhetoric* 'before even I knew that he had translated any part of it, for I found the 2 first books englished by him in the hands of the noble, studious Henry Wotton but lately'. Nothing further is known of this version's fate.

# CHAPTER XXIV

# SIDNEY AND DON ANTONIO – FAMILY
# LETTERS – MARRIAGE

Literature, whether in prose or verse, fictional or autobiographical, could not entirely occupy Sidney in the early eighties. He was elected a Member of Parliament, though the constituency is not known, in 1581, and served on two important Committees before the Queen, alarmed at the increasing independence of tone of the House of Commons, prorogued Parliament on March 18th. Sidney had meanwhile on New Year's Day made a peace offering to her of 'a jewel of gold, being a whip, garnished with small diamonds in four rows and cords of small seed pearls'. A few months later an opportunity offered of making a more striking display of his personal loyalty. Circumstances had led to a revival of the project of a marriage between Elizabeth and D'Alençon, now the Duke of Anjou. French commissioners to complete the negotiations arrived in April and were sumptuously entertained. In spite of Sidney's strong opposition to the match, he may have felt that it was useless to go against the Queen's apparent decision in its favour. In any case, he may well have planned, and certainly took a prominent part in, the most elaborate of the ceremonial shows, on Whit Monday and Tuesday. The gallery in the tilt-yard at Whitehall was fitted up as the Castle or Fortress of Perfect Beauty and it was attacked by four 'Foster Children of Desire', represented by the Earl of Arundel, Lord Windsor, Sidney and Fulke Greville. Sidney had indulged his lavish tastes to the utmost in his outfit. He was arrayed in

> armour part blue and the rest gilt and engraven, with four
> spare horses having caparisons and furniture very rich and
> costly, as some of cloth of gold embroidered with pearl,
> and some embroidered with gold and silver feathers very

richly and cunningly wrought. He had four pages that
rode on his four spare horses, who had cassock coats and
Venetian hose of all cloth of silver laid with gold lace, and
hats of the same with gold bands and white feathers, and
each one a pair of white buskins. Then had he a thirty
gentlemen and yeomen and four trumpeters.

No wonder that Sidney was constantly in want of money.

The defenders of the castle, where the Queen was en-
throned, refused to surrender, and ran six courses against
the Foster-Children of Desire, each side performing valiant
feats. The encounter was renewed on the following day with
similar valiancy till towards evening when the attackers ten-
dered their submission and the Queen thanked all who had
taken part. But once more she would not commit herself to
a betrothal and, doubtless to Sidney's relief, the negotiations
again came to nought. Nevertheless the Duke again visited
England in October, when Elizabeth encouraged him by
kissing him and giving him a ring. But nothing further came
of their contact, and Sidney was chosen as part of the escort
to Anjou on his return journey. His death in May 1583
brought to a close something of a prolonged tragi-comedy.

Meanwhile Sidney had become involved in the affairs of
another foreign royalty, Don Antonio, claimant to the throne
of Portugal, which Philip of Spain had assumed on the death
of the Cardinal-King on January 31st, 1580. It suited the
policy of both England and France to give promise of support to Antonio in opposition to the ambitious despotism of
Philip, and with this policy Sidney was in eager accord. He
probably saw Antonio when he paid a first visit to London
in 1580, to make preliminary plans for an expedition with
Drake to the Azores. Before paying a second visit in June
1581 Antonio wrote to Sidney on May 13th, 1581, from
Tunis, addressing him as *Al Illustre Filipe Cidenci mi
amado Sobrino*, and stressing the importance of his presence
in the expedition. But the French King, Henri III, would
take no active steps and, though Elizabeth allowed Antonio
to fit out a fleet at Plymouth, she refused permission to
Drake to sail with him. Towards the end of September he
left London, and was accompanied by Sidney on most of

the way to Dover. Thence on September 26th he wrote in impatient mood to Hatton:

> The delay of this Prince's departure is so long as truly I grow very weary of it, having divers businesses of my own and my father's that something import me, and to deal plainly with you, being grown almost to the bottom of my purse. Therefore your Honour shall do me a singular favour if you can find means to send for me away . . .I durst not depart without her [Highness'] special revocation and commandment.

At last Antonio's wind-bound ships were able to set sail, and by October 10th Sidney was back in London, when he wrote to Burghley telling him that on taking leave of the Queen, she said 'she would take some order for me. I told her Majesty I would beseech your Lordship to have some care of me therein. Her Majesty seemed then to like better of some present matter of relief than the expecting the office. Truly, Sir, so do I too.'

A month later he was again writing to Hatton begging him to present to the Queen a book prepared for her signature entitling him to some office. 'If you find you cannot prevail, I beseech you let me know it as soon as may be, for I will even shamelessly once in my life bring it her Majesty myself. Need obeys no laws and forgets blushing.' These last words must have left their sting in Sidney's breast when he wrote again to Hatton on December 18th. The Queen evidently had disappointed his hope of the desired office, but had offered him a sum to relieve his necessities from the fines on recusants.

> Some of my friends counsel me to stand upon her Majesty's offer, touching the forfeiture of papists' goods; truly, Sir, I know not how to be more sure of her Highness in that than I thought myself in this. But, though I were, in truth it goeth against my heart to prevent a Prince's mercy: my necessity is great.

Ten days later on December 28th, in a letter to the Earl of Leicester he showed himself doubtful whether the Queen will stand even by her offer:

I know not truly what to say since her Majesty is pleased
so to answer, for as well may her Majesty refuse the matter
of the papists, and then have I both shame and scorn. I
beseech your Lordship resolve of it with Mr Vice-Chamberlain . . . But this I beseech your Lordship without it
be 3000ˡⁱ never to trouble yourself in it . . . Truly I like
not their persons and much worse their religions, but I
think my fortunes very hard that my reward must be built
upon other men's punishments.

The last words do credit to Sidney's feelings but they did
not prevent him from accepting the money. Professor Wallace draws attention[1] to an undated Note, in the Domestic
State Papers for 1583, 'of money leviable upon the Recusants
and Clergy with appoint of part of the produce to the Earl
of Leicester, Sir Thomas Cecil and Sir Philip Sidney'. The
two latter had already received £2,000 and were to receive
£1,000 more. This was the sum mentioned by Sidney to
Leicester as his minimum requirement.

A pleasanter aspect of Sidney's correspondence during
this period is to be found in his purely domestic letters,
especially to his brother Robert, his junior by nine years.
Robert had followed him to Christ Church and afterwards
to temporary residence on the Continent. Sir Henry had
indeed enjoined upon him to take his elder brother as a
model in every way. Seldom can a father have given such an
unreserved testimonial to a son.

> Follow the direction of your most loving brother who
> in loving you is comparable with me or exceedeth me.
> Imitate his virtues, exercises, studies and actions; he is a
> rare ornament of this age, the very formular that all well-
> disposed young gentlemen of our Court do form also their
> manners and life by. In truth I speak it without flattery
> of him or of myself: he hath the most rare virtues that
> ever I found in any man.

Robert had dutifully asked Philip to give him the benefit of
his experience as a traveller, and in an undated letter Philip
had replied in characteristic fashion.

[1] Op. cit., p. 272.

Your purpose is, being a Gentleman born, to furnish yourself with the knowledge of such things as may be serviceable to your country and fit for your calling, which certainly stands not in the change of air, for the warmest sun makes not a wise man, no more in learning languages (although they be of good serviceable case), for words are but words in what language soever they be . . . but in the right informing your mind with those things which are most notable in those places you come to . . . for hard sure it is to know England without you know it by comparing it with others, no more than a man can know the swiftness of his horse without seeing him well matched . . . so as you cannot tell what the Queen of England is able to do, defensively, or offensively, but by through comparing what they are able to do with whom she is to be matched.

Are not these last words as propheticably apt in the reign of Elizabeth II as of Elizabeth I? Even some of the details into which Philip goes for his brother's benefit concerning different countries are still relevant, as is his parting injunction on 'the chiefest' of all points, 'the choice of what men you are to addict yourself unto to learn these things . . . and try well what you have heard before you hold it for a principle, for one error is the mother of a thousand'.

Another letter, dated October 18th, 1580, and signed 'from your most loving and careful brother, Philip Sidney', goes into more intimate detail. Robert evidently had felt that he had been making excessive demands upon Philip's slender purse, for the latter begins 'My dear brother, for the money you have received, assure yourself (for it is true) there is nothing I spend so pleaseth me as that which is for you. If ever I have ability, you will find it; if not, yet shall not any brother living be better beloved than you of me.' Then in connexion with Robert's studies Philip enters into a lengthy analysis of the various functions of a historian which might have found a place in *The Defence of Poesie*. Even so, he apologizes for writing in great haste, but with more leisure he 'will venture to write more largely of it'. Yet he finds time to admonish Robert on a number of other studies and pursuits. He is to 'take delight in the mathematicals'. 'I think you understand the sphere; if you do, I care little for any more astronomy in you. Arithmetic and geometry I would wish you well seen in.'

There follows a somewhat remarkable passage. 'So you can speak and write Latin, not barbarously, I never require great study in Circeronianism, the chief abuse of Oxford, *Qui dum verba sectantur, res ipsas negligunt*. It is curious that in one of his few references to Oxford Sidney should speak disparagingly of it, and that the author of the highly patterned Arcadian style should disapprove of the academic attempts to emulate the rhetorical embellishments of Cicero. Then this zigzag epistle returns to the subject of Robert's finances, and goes off again abruptly to the improvement of his accomplishments. 'Now, sweet brother, take a delight to keep and increase your music: you will not believe what a want I find of it in my melancholy times.' When exercising horsemanship he will greatly speed up his mastery of it by reading certain treatises on it. Then comes suddenly the half-playful admonition, 'I would by the way, your worship would learn a better hand, you write worse than I, and I write evil enough; once again take care of your diet, and consequently of your complexion; remember, *Gratior est veniens in pulchro corpore virtus*.' It is the Renaissance ideal of virtue clothed in suitably beautiful form, towards which daily practice with weapons for the tilt-yard will contribute. It is indeed a comprehensive cultural and physical programme, into which slips as an incidental piece of information, 'Nothing is happened notable at home, save only Drake's return, of which yet I know not the secret points, but about the world he hath been, and rich he is returned.'

These letters help to show how close were the bonds between members of the Sidney family, but Philip was now about to form the most intimate of ties with another family of the first rank. Sir Francis Walsingham, the Queen's principal Secretary of State, had always looked upon him with favour. By his second wife, whom he had married in 1566, he had a daughter, Frances, now about fourteen years of age. It is difficult to think of the Astrophel of the Sonnets paying his suit to so youthful a 'teenager' in modern parlance, and mixing it up with his family's financial straits. But there appears to be no doubt that in the following letter of Sidney to Walsingham on December 17th, 1581, from Wilton he is referring in a discreet subterfuge to his bride-to-be.

The country affords no other stuff for letters but humble salutations, which indeed humbly and heartily I send to yourself, my good Lady, and my exceeding like to be good friend. I will be bold to add herewith the beseeching you to favour this bearer that he may have some consideration for the packet he brought, because belonging to my brother Robert, a younger brother of so youngly a fortuned family as the Sidneys. I am sure, at least I have very vehement conjectures, that he is more stored with discourses than money.

It is to be hoped that Robert's servant obtained the requested gratuity. But a considerable time was to elapse before Philip and Frances were made husband and wife. There is no further reference to the subject in Philip's extant letters written in 1582. On February 18th, 1583, Burghley wrote to Walsingham, 'I hear of the comfortable purpose toward for your daughter, God bless it; as I would any of my own so is that great hope.' To speak of a union with Philip Sidney as a 'comfortable purpose' was in its financial aspect something of a misuse of terms, though Sir Henry had made a will settling upon the pair most of his property, and he and Sir Francis had entered into an agreement, including a tell-tale informal stipulation that 'the said Sir Francis is well contented and will undertake to pay or discharge the debts of the said Sir Philip so far as shall amount unto £1,500, and will allow to the said Sir Philip and Mrs Frances and their servants their diet if they will take it with him and in his house'. It will be noted that here for the first time in any reference cited in this narrative is 'Sir' prefixed to Philip, and of a truth he was the embodiment of many knightly qualities. But it is one of the paradoxes of his career that it was not on account of them or of his achievements in any sphere that he received the accolade. It was merely that he might act as the Elector Casimir's proxy at an installation of Garter Knights at Windsor in January 1583.

During the protracted negotiations no one had informed

the Queen of the projected match and when it came to her
ears she was highly indignant. Sir Francis, writing on March
19th, 1583, to thank Sir Christopher Hatton who had taken
the lead in the defence of the match, continued:

> I find it strange that her Majesty should be offended
> withal. It is either to proceed of the matter or of the man-
> ner. For the matter, I hope when Her Majesty shall weigh
> the due circumstances of place, person and quality, there
> can grow no just cause of offence: if the manner be mis-
> liked, for that her Majesty is not made acquainted withal,
> I am no person of that state but that it may be thought a
> presumption for me to trouble Her Majesty with a private
> marriage between a free gentleman of equal calling with
> my daughter. I had well hoped that my painful and faith-
> ful service done unto Her Majesty had merited that grace
> and favour at her hands, as that she would have coun-
> tenanced this match with her gracious and princely good
> liking thereof, that thereby the world might have been a
> witness of her goodness towards me.

Elizabeth, however, is scarcely to be blamed if, with her
memory of Northumberland's *coup d'état*, she felt that she
ought to be informed of a projected alliance of a gifted man
of Dudley blood, a nephew of the Earl of Leicester, with the
daughter of one of her most powerful ministers. In any case
she refused to give the Sidney family any concrete reward
for their services. As Sir Henry wrote to Walsingham on
March 1583,

> As I know, Sir, that it is the virtue which is, or that
> you suppose is, in my son that you made choice of him
> for your daughter, refusing haply far greater and far
> richer matches than he, so was my confidence great that
> by your good means I might have obtained some small
> reasonable suit of her Majesty; and therefore I nothing
> regard any present gain, for if I had, I might have received
> a great sum of money for my good will of my son's mar-
> riage, greatly to the relief of my private, biting necessity.

Elizabeth relented sufficiently after a time for the marriage to take place on September 21st, 1583, after which the

pair took up their residence, in accordance with the stipulation mentioned above, with the Walsingham family. That helps to account for the fact that the record of their married life is almost a complete blank, though biographers on general grounds seem to be warranted in assuming that it is a case of no news being good news.

# CHAPTER XXV

# OXFORD AGAIN – TRANS-ATLANTIC ENTER-PRISE – ORDNANCE OFFICE – SIDNEY AND DRAKE

Earlier in this year Sidney had given a courteous welcome to the Italian philosopher, Giordano Bruno, who had arrived in England in the hope of spreading the revolutionary astronomical doctrines of Copernicus. But though Bruno dedicated two of his dialogues, *Spaccio de la Bestia Triofante* and *De Gli Heroici Furori* to Sidney, with very flattering references to him and to Greville, there is no evidence of his having influenced Sidney's cosmic views. And during a three months' residence in Oxford, if his account is to be believed, the Dons displayed towards him a mixture of stupidity and spite. Very different was the University's attitude towards another foreign visitor for a few days, the Polish Prince, Albertus Alasco. The Earl of Leicester, as Chancellor of the University, had announced that the 'Lasky' would arrive, accompanied by himself, on June 10th, 1583, and was to be entertained 'with all solemnity of disputations, orations, and readings', as on Elizabeth's visit in 1566. William Gager of Christ Church, who had gained a success in February 1581 with his Latin play, *Meleager*,[1] a tragedy on the same theme as Swinburne's *Atalanta in Calydon*, was commissioned to write for performance before the royal visitor a comedy, *Rivales*, and a tragedy, *Dido*. As far as is known, Sidney did not accompany his uncle on this occasion, as he had done during his schooldays, though on Alasco's return journey he was one of his company on a visit to the astrologer, Dr. John Dee. It was not till a year and half later, in January 1584–5, that Sidney and Pembroke accompanied Leicester when he paid another official visit to the University, and they attended a revival of *Meleager*. This is clear from a

[1] Professor Wallace is mistaken in stating, op. cit., p. 267, that this play was then seen by the Earls of Pembroke and Leicester and Philip Sidney. It was the revival which was thus honoured.

passage in Gager's dedication of the play to the Earl of
Essex, when in January 1592–3 it was printed at the Oxford
University Press.

> Annus jam pene undecimus agitur . . . ex quo Meleager
> primum, octavus ex quo iterum in Scenam venit: primum
> quidem violens ac sponte suà; trienno post, invitatus,
> publicque evocatas, secundum prodiit, assedentibus ac
> spectantibus clarissimis Comitibus Pembrochiensi ae
> Lecestrensi, Cancellario tum mostro, unà cum nobilissimo
> Philippo Sidnaeo nonnullisqie illustribus Aulicis.

For the first performance of *Meleager* Gager had provided
a prologue and epilogue 'ad Academicos'; for the revival he
added two others addressed to Leicester and Pembroke in
which he declared he would be satisfied if they were pleased,
and

> Si spes Philippus nostra Sidnaeus probet,
> Ubicumque sedeat ille, qui solus novis
> Favet poetis, ipse vates optimus,
> Meleager ipse noster: a verbis meis
> Triste absit omen, et procul fatis suis.
> Miscrandus absit, opto, Meleagri exitus.

Gager doubtless wished to pay a special tribute to a distinguished son of the 'House', but it is curious that he should
single out Sidney as the only favourer of new poets, and
that after his untimely death the ill-omened reference to
'Meleagri exitus' should have been made public.

In Sidney's letter of October 19th, 1580, to his brother
he had alluded to Drake's return from his voyage round the
world, and his interest in overseas expeditions, already shown
in connexion with Frobisher, received further stimulus during this period of comparative public unemployment. Besides
his Renaissance zest for adventurous exploration, he had two
motives for supporting schemes of English settlement in the
New World. They promised a counterpoise to the Spanish
monopoly of power there, and they offered an economical
means of finding habitation for recusants. In June 1578 the
Queen had granted to Sir Humphrey Gilbert letters patent
for the planting of an English colony in America. Finding

difficulty in raising funds for such an enterprise Gilbert after
a time conceived the plan of selling the rights in American
soil granted him by the letters patent. The chief purchasers
were two prominent Roman Catholics, Sir George Peckham
and Sir Thomas Gurney. Philip Sidney and his father also
took shares and the former covenanted to use his best en-
deavours to get the Queen to grant liberty to members of the
expedition to remain or return, as they pleased. For Sir
Humphrey, drowned on September 9th, 1582, there was
to be no return, and Sidney had already sold his rights to
Peckham. But it is curious that as late as July 21st, 1584,
he should write to Sir Edward Stafford, the English ambassador at the French Court, 'We are half persuaded to
enter into the journey of Sir Humphrey Gilbert very eagerly,
whereunto your Mr Hakluyt hath served for a very good
trumpet.'

Another preoccupation of Sidney during this period was
to have a more fortunate, though delayed, issue. His uncle,
the Earl of Warwick, Master of the Ordnance, was anxious
to have his nephew associated with him in the office. On
January 27th, 1582-3, Philip wrote to Burghley, stating
that, as he learns, 'her Majesty yields gracious hearing' unto
the proposal, and asking the Lord Treasurer to favour and
further it. Yet on July 20th Sidney is again craving Burghley's good word 'for the confirming that grant she once made
unto me of joining me patent with my lord of Warwick,
whose desire is that it should be so'. Nevertheless he was
given only a subordinate appointment and it was not till
July 21st, 1585, that he was appointed Joint Master.

At the Ordnance Office he had the congenial task of
helping in the defence preparations against the ever-growing
threat of an invasion by Spain. And his abilities as a pen-
man were enlisted in his reply to the scurrilous pamphlet
*Leicester's Commonwealth*, which formed part of the pro-
paganda against Elizabeth, and which represented the Earl
as being the virtual governor of England. It was thought
necessary to draw up a Bond of Association of which the
signatories bound themselves to destroy anyone who attempted an assault on the Queen. To legalize the Bond it
was necessary to summon a new Parliament which met on

November 23rd, 1584. In this Parliament Sidney served on
a number of Committees, including one on a Bill for confirming letters patent to Walter Raleigh for the land in
Virginia.

On this Committee one of his colleagues was Drake and
Sidney was soon brought otherwise into close association
with him. A commission was signed on Christmas Eve,
1584, for Drake to lead an expedition to the West Indies,
and one of the military commanders under him was to be
Christopher Carleill, another son-in-law of Walsingham.
Sidney saw in the expedition a favourable opportunity of
attacking Spain in her overseas possessions and aspired to
be general of its land forces. But the whole affair hung fire
till in June 1585 an English ship, the *Primrose*, reported
that she had been treacherously attacked while lying off
Bilbao by two Spaniards who had come aboard her in friendly
guise. Drake was at once given authority to requisition ships
for his enterprise.

About the same time a kindred one was being set on foot.
Under the terms of the Bill for Virginia, Sir Richard Gren-
ville had sailed with a body of planters in the spring, and had
left Ralph Lane at Roanoke as Governor of the colony. Lane
wrote to Sidney on August 12th to say that the power of the
Spanish King had been greatly exaggerated and 'to exhort
you, my noble general, by occasion not to refuse the good
opportunity of such a service to the Church of Christ, of
great relief from many calamities that this treasure in Spanish
hands doth inflict unto the members thereof, very honourable and profitable for her Majesty and our country, and
most commendable and fit for yourself to be the enterpriser
thereof'.

Saluting Sidney as 'noble general' Lane would seem to
have assumed that he had been appointed to an official command in connexion with the expedition. But apparently
Elizabeth had not been approached, when at the end of
August Drake sent a message from Plymouth to Sidney to
the effect that his fleet was ready to sail. Sidney and Fulke
Greville at once set out for Plymouth, and were received, as
Greville records, 'with a great deal of outward pomp and
compliment'. But Greville noticed that Drake was troubled,

'as if our coming were both beyond his expectation and desire'. And so indeed it was. The fleet was still delayed, and Sir Francis wrote to the Queen concerning Philip's presence and his aims. She ordered the Vice-Chamberlain to summon him back to London, and when his letters were disregarded, an ultimatum was delivered through a peer of the realm recalling him immediately and announcing that he had been appointed Governor of Flushing. Unlike Gilbert, or Drake himself, it was not with the high seas or the West Indies, that the well-nigh legendary fame of his last days was to be associated.

To add to the complication of Sidney's affairs, he was involved in the tangled relations of the English Court with Scotland. A number of Protestant Lords, headed by the Earl of Angus, had attempted unsuccessfully to deprive the Earl of Arran of his controlling influence over James VI. They had fled to England, and the Master of Grey was sent to demand their expulsion. But he was untrustworthy, and when he reached London he pleaded the cause of the exiled nobles to Elizabeth. She, however, did not reply, and she made difficulties about paying a pension of £5,000 which had been promised to James. Sidney induced Leicester to provide part of the sum. He had previously become friendly with Angus, and it may have been partly on this account that the burden of entertaining the Scottish Lords was laid upon 'poor Sir Philip Sidney', as Walsingham called him. In the prolonged negotiations that followed he played a leading part, and James showed him 'many pledges of love and favour'. Sidney must have welcomed the ratification of a league between England and Scotland in December 1585.

Before that date the Queen had given another sign of her good will for the time being to Sidney by consenting to act as godmother to his infant daughter who was christened Elizabeth at St. Olave's Church, Hart Street, on November 20th, 1585. The Queen came up from Richmond for the ceremony, and amidst the clash of international negotiations it is pleasant to hear the domestic note of an allowance of 100 shillings in the royal household accounts to a gentleman of the chamber to be distributed by way of her Majesty's reward to the nurse and midwife at the christening of Sir

Philip Sidney's daughter. Sidney himself had already left for the Netherlands. On November 10th he had written to the Queen from Gravesend enclosing a cipher for which she had stipulated, promising to let her know any news sufficiently important to be 'so marked' and beseeching her in almost Arcadian phrase 'legibly to read my heart in the course of my life, and though itself be but of a mean worth, yet to esteem it like a poor house well set'.

# CHAPTER XXVI

# GOVERNOR OF FLUSHING – PESSIMIST REPORT – ARRIVAL OF LEICESTER – DEATH OF SIR HENRY AND LADY MARY

Accompanied by his brother Robert, the new Governor reached Flushing after an uncomfortable journey on November 18th, 1585, and on November 21st took an oath of fidelity to the States. Flushing was the most important of the 'contingency towns' which Elizabeth had exacted from the Netherlands as the price of her support against Spain. Had this support been whole-hearted, Sidney's post would have given him special opportunities for the display of his abilities. But as he revealed in a letter to his uncle Leicester four days after his arrival, the conditions that he found were very disturbing.

> I find the people very glad of me . . . the garrison is far too weak to command by authority, which is pity for how great a jewel this is to the Crown of England and the Queen's safety I need not write it to your Lordship who knows it so well. Yet I must needs say the better I know it, the more I find the preciousness of it.

*     *     *

> Mr Edward Norris delivered the companies here unto me whom he had very well and soldierly governed, but the companies indeed very sickly and miserable. Good my lord, haste away if you do come, for all things considered I had rather you came not at all than came not quickly, for only by your own presence those sources can be stopped which, if they run on, will be past remedy . . . I think truly, if my coming had been longer delayed, some alteration would have followed, for the truth is the people is weary of war, and if they do not see such a course taken as may be likely to defend them, they will in a sudden give over the cause.

Sidney had good cause for his pessimism. The English garrison was inadequate in numbers, was badly accommodated, and two hundred of them were sick in hospital. The fortifications of the town were in very bad repair and unable to resist any powerful attack. How anxious Sidney was to conciliate the townsfolk is seen from a letter that he sent by a messenger to Walsingham on November 23rd:

This is a burghess of Flushing who now begins to take the benefit of her Majesty's grant unto them, which in her Majesty's name I have assured them of, namely that they shall be as custom free as English born subjects, for such be the words of the instructions. I humbly beseech you to give orders that both he and all such that come with like certificate from me may be well used, for else were such a blow to my credit as I should never recover.

In order to meet the necessities of some of his ill-paid troops he borrowed £300 'at usance' from a banking firm, and begged Walsingham to see that the day of repayment be observed, 'that I may preserve my credit in these parts'. He also protested to Walsingham on December 14th against the payment to the troops in the province of Zeeland in a coinage 'which is 5. in the 100 loss to the poor soldiers who, God knows, want no such hindrances, being scarce able to keep life with their entire pay'.

Meanwhile, on December 10th, the Earl of Leicester, on whose coming such high hopes were based, had arrived in Flushing where he was received by Count Maurice, son of William of Orange and by Sidney. After spending a day there the Earl made a progress in which he was sumptuously entertained and was offered by the States-General the office of Governor-General, which after some hesitation he accepted on January 14th, 1586. Hence arose further complications. Elizabeth had given Leicester express instructions not to accept the Governor-Generalship, and was at first furious when he sent William Davison to announce and explain the step that he had taken. She drafted an order to Leicester to resign the office, but it was delayed, and meanwhile the chief Ministers and the Privy Council stood by Leicester. Elizabeth, thereupon, turned part of her anger against Davison and Sidney, whom she accused of being 'principal actors and persuaders' in the matter, though the Earl had proceeded on his own initiative. Sidney, however, was more concerned for his uncle than himself. In the course of a long letter on February 19th, 1586, to him on various aspects of the general situation he writes, giving him his new title:

> I beseech your Excellency be not discouraged with the Queen's discontentments, for the event being any thing good, your glory will shine through those mists, only if it please you to have daily counsel taken of your means, how to increase them and how to husband them. And when all is said, if they can serve, you shall make a noble war; if not, the peace is in your hand.

But Sidney in this last sentence was to find himself too optimistic. News of the Queen's attitude to Leicester had reached the States-General, and undermined his influence, and when Sir Thomas Heneage arrived in the Netherlands with her modified reproofs, Sidney reported from Amsterdam to Burghley on March 18th that he 'hath with as much honesty, in my opinion, done as much hurt as any man this twelve month hath done with naughtiness, but I hope in God when her Majesty finds the truth of things, her graciousness will not utterly overthrow a cause so behoveful and costly unto her'.

This was followed on March 25th by a letter from Sidney at Utrecht to Walsingham, which is of special interest for various reasons. Philip begs his father-in-law not to be troubled because part of the Queen's displeasure had fallen on him.

> I had before cast my count of danger, want and disgrace, and before God, Sir, it is true that in my heart the love of the cause doth so far overbalance them all that with God's grace they shall never make me weary of my resolution. If her Majesty were the fountain I would fear, considering what I daily find, that we should wax dry but she is but a means whom God useth, and I know not whether I am deceived, but I am faithfully persuaded that if she should withdraw herself, other springs would rise to help this

action. For, methinks, I see the great work indeed in hand against the abusers of the world, wherein it is no greater fault to have confidence in man's power than it is too hastily to despair of God's work . . . Because I know there is a higher power that must uphold me or else I shall fall; but certainly, I trust, I shall not by other men's counts be drawn from myself.

This is the most categorical avowal by Sidney of the religious faith which was the mainspring of his actions, and it is characteristic of the practical side of his idealism that he shortly afterwards adds, 'If the Queen pay not her soldiers, she must lose her garrisons, there is no doubt thereof.'

Then comes a uniquely explicit reference by Sidney to his wife. 'For Bergen ap Zoom I delighted in it, I confess, because it was near the enemy, but especially having a very fair house in it and an excellent air, I destined it for my wife . . . but considering how apt the Queen is to interpret every thing to my disadvantage, I have resigned it to my Lord Willoughby, my very friend.' In a postscript he adds, 'I know not what to say to my wife's coming till you resolve better, for if you run a strange course, I may take such a one here as will not be fit for any of the feminine gender.' What a contrast, even if no significance was intended, between this grammatical classification of Frances and the rhapsodies over Stella!

There follows an unexpected tantalizing inquiry:
I wrote to you a letter by William, My Lord of Leicester's jesting player, enclosed in a letter to my wife, and I never had answer thereof; it contained something to my Lord of Leicester, and counsel that some way might be taken to stay my Lady there. I since divers times have writ to know whether you have received them, but you never answered me that point. I since find that the knave delivered the letters to my Lady of Leicester but whether she sent them you or no I know not, but earnestly desire to do, because I doubt there is more interpreted thereof.

In Sidney's words we 'earnestly desire' that he had given William's surname, though the chances are that he was

Kempe, who had been in Dunkirk in the autumn of 1585. But, whether Kempe or another, why should Sidney with official machinery at his disposal have employed one of his uncle's comedians to carry letters, including one which urged that the Countess should not join her husband, lest this should be misinterpreted by Elizabeth, and the apparent miscarriage of which troubled Sidney sorely? We would gladly know more of his relations with this 'knave' than with some of his highly titled correspondents.

Letter-writing must have occupied much of his time. In April he sent three epistles in French to the States of Zeeland on military and political matters. He tried to soothe the hurt feelings of Davison whom Leicester had accused of having 'utterly and with tears disclaimed' him concerning the Governor-Generalship. 'These mistakings sometimes breed hard effects, but I know he in his judgement loves you very well, howsoever in his passion he have written.' His zeal for discipline appears in a letter to Walsingham on May 6th. Four soldiers of Captain Huntley's regiment had run away to England, though they had been as well used by him as any men might be. 'I beseech your Honour give orders they may be sent back again, for else we shall have the like villainy used, and some back out of England will save us from the like again.' Another letter to Walsingham on May 10th is of a more personal nature. Sidney recommends the bearer of it to his father-in-law as 'one of excellent skill proved by most notable cures he hath done . . . He healed Roger Williams in three days when for my part I thought he would have been dead in three days'. But Sidney is anxious that before his expert undertakes the case of Walsingham he makes proof of his hand and skill on other patients in England. And he adds: 'He is an Anabaptist in religion which is pity, for in conversation[1] he is honest.'

A few days before this letter was written, one who was even closer to Sidney than his father-in-law had passed beyond the help of any human practitioner. On May 5th Sir Henry Sidney, worn out by the ill-requited cares of office at the age of fifty-six, had died in the Bishop's palace in Worcester. His heart was buried in the oratory of the Lud-

[1] Conduct.

low Parish Church, his entrails in Worcester Cathedral; and his body was escorted by 140 horsemen, members of the Welsh Council, and others connected with him to Penshurst, where it was laid in the Church on June 21st. With her curiously churlish behaviour to the Sidney family the Queen refused an application for Philip to return to England to settle his father's affairs and to see his mother. Lady Mary had for long been in failing health. Bereft of her husband, and with her sons absent in the Netherlands, she ended a saintly life on August 9th and was laid beside her husband in Penshurst Church. Soon after Sir Henry's funeral Sidney had the consolation of being joined by his wife. He writes to Walsingham from Utrecht on June 28th, 'I am presently going toward Flushing whence I learn that your daughter is very well and merry.' It is scarcely the adjective that in all the circumstances might have been expected.

# CHAPTER XXVII

## MILITARY OPERATIONS – WOUNDED AT ZUTPHEN – MAKES WILL – DEATH

Meanwhile in the spring of 1586 Leicester's forces had shown some successful activity. The Duke of Parma was laying siege to the town of Grave. The Earl commissioned Sir John Norris and Count Hohenlo to relieve it, which they brilliantly accomplished, and supplied it with a year's victuals. Leicester saw in this operation the happiest of omens for his campaign. But Parma returned to the attack, and on June 7th the commandant most unexpectedly surrendered. This was followed in three weeks by the capture of Venloo, and in August by that of Neuss. On the other hand, forces under Sidney, Lord Willoughby and Prince Maurice succeeded in taking Axel in a night attack early in July, without the loss of a single man. But a disaster soon followed. News was brought to Sidney that the garrison of Gravelines was ready to hand over the town to him. This turned out to be a trap, and though Sidney had cautiously sent in advance a body of about eighty men, rather more than half of them were lost. To Sidney's chagrin over this 'flat treason' as he calls it, was added the persistent harassing need of appealing for fresh supplies of men and money. Thus on August 14th he sends to the English Council a Mr Burnam

to give your Lordships to understand the weak store of all sort of necessary munition that both this town and the castle of Ramekins have . . . By the grace of God my trust is in him that my life shall discharge me of blame, but I nor all that be here can perform the service we owe to her Majesty without such merely necessary things . . . There is nothing will keep these people in better order than that they see we are strong.

On the same day he wrote twice to Walsingham, asking him to confer with Burnam, and to 'labour for me or rather for Her Majesty in it. She need not be discouraged with no thing while she keeps these principal sea places . . . we do still make camps and straight again mar them for want of means, and so lose our money to no purpose.' In the second letter he is even more explicit:

> I often crave the Treasurer might be commanded to pay this place. I assure you, Sir, this night we were at a fair plunge to have lost all for want of it. We are now four months behind, a thing insupportable in this place. To complain of my Lord of Leicester you know I may not, but this is the case, if once the soldiers fall to a thorough mutiny, this town is lost in all likelihood. I did never think our nation had been so apt to go to the enemy as I find them.

He added a fourth letter to Burghley, 'in great haste because the ship can stay no longer', in which he besought him to hear from Mr Burnam 'in what case for all sort of munition we are in this town. I think Sir Thomas Cecil [in Brill] be in the like . . . The garrison is weak, the people by their crass fortunes crossly disposed; and this is the conclusion, if these 2 places be kept, her Majesty hath worth her money in all extremities; if they should be lost, none of the rest would hold a day.'

In all these letters Sidney's devotion to the interest of the Queen is apparent. Yet Walsingham reported to Leicester, 'I see her Majesty very apt upon every light occasion to find fault with him'. On the other hand, in Flushing, he had the loving reverence of all men. But soon he was to be out of the reach of earthly blame or praise. After the capture of Neuss, Parma besieged Berek. In the hope of forcing him to raise the siege the Earl decided to invest the town of Doesburg. On September 2nd two breaches in the walls were made, and the town capitulated. Sidney, who had taken part in the operations, must have strongly disapproved of the ruthless way in which, in spite of Leicester's orders, the city was put to the sack.

Parma thereupon returned to the siege of Berek, and to divert him again, Leicester on September 13th turned to the neighbourhood of Zutphen which lay about equidistant from Doesburg and Deventer. As the allegiance of the latter town was doubtful, Leicester, accompanied by Sidney, paid it a visit. While there, Sidney on September 14th wrote a Latin letter to his scholar friend, Justus Lipsius, asking him to come back, expressing anxiety about his health, and promising to help Paul Bus, whose fidelity had become suspect. Sidney's last English letter, about a week later, to Walsingham was characteristically on behalf of an old servant of her Majesty, Richard Smyth. 'I beseech you . . . be the good mean for the poor man's preferment, having so long served, and now being aged and weak hath such need of this or such other good mean for his relief, as without it he may rest, as I hear, in more misery than the desert of such a service requireth.'

This letter was written from the camp at Zutphen, to which Sidney had returned with Leicester. The town stood on the right bank of the river Yssel; on the left bank were two very strong forts. Leicester laid siege to both the town and the forts. He undertook himself the reduction of the latter and he sent Sir John Norris, accompanied by Sidney, across the river to invest the town. From a Spanish prisoner it was learnt that Parma was sending a convoy of provisions into Zutphen, and Leicester thought that this would have only a comparatively small escort. He ordered Norris to prepare an ambuscade of 500 men, and these were joined by about fifty gallants from Leicester's own force. A fog hid the approach of the Spanish relieving force, and when it lifted this was found to number 3,000 foot and 1,500 horse. With reckless bravery the English cavalry charged again and again against these overwhelming odds, but had to recoil from the muskets of the Spanish footmen in ambush in their own trenches. After a comparatively short engagement the English withdrew with small casualties which, in part being his own act, included Sidney. This moving climax to his life's drama has been immortalized in Greville's account. Sidney had put on his full armour, but meeting the elderly Sir William Pelham, the Lord Marshal, without his thigh-pieces, 'to venture without any inequality' he decided to cast off his own 'and so by the secret influence of destiny, to disarm that part where God (it seems) had resolved to strike him'. For after one horse had been shot under him, as he was charging a second time, a musket-shot broke the bone of his unprotected thigh, and he had to ride off the field to the camp.

In which sad progress, passing along by the rest of the army, where his uncle, the General, was, and being thirsty with excess of bleeding, he called for drink, which was presently[1] brought him; but as he was putting the bottle to his mouth he saw a poor soldier carried along, who had eaten his last at the same feast, ghastly casting up his eyes at the bottle. Which Sir Philip perceiving, took it from his head before he drank, and delivered it to the poor man with these words, 'Thy necessity is yet greater than mine.' And when he had pledged this poor soldier, he was presently carried to Arnheim.

Leicester was grief-stricken at his nephew's dangerous plight. He wrote to Sir Thomas Heneage next day:

This young man he was my greatest comfort, next her Majesty, of all the world, and if I could buy his life with all I have, to my shirt, I would give it. How God will dispose of him I know not, but fear I must needs greatly the worst, the blow in so dangerous a place and so great; yet never did I hear of any man that did abide the dressing and setting his bones better than he did. And he was carried afterwards in my barge to Arnheim, and I hear this day he is still of good heart and comforteth all about him as much as may be. God in his mercy grant me his life which I cannot but doubt of greatly.

For a time it seemed as if Leicester's prayer was to be favourably answered. He lingered for sixteen days, and, in Greville's words, the doctors had 'such confidence of his recovery as the joy of their hearts overflowed their discretion, and made them to spread the intelligence of it to the Queen and all his noble friends here in England, where it was received not as private but public good news'.

As late as October 6th Leicester reported to Walsingham that Philip 'is well amending as ever any man hath done for so short time. He feeleth no grief now but his long lying,

[1] Immediately.

which he must suffer. His wife is with him, and I to-morrow am going to him for a start.'

Sidney himself did not share this confidence in his recovery. On September 30th he took advantage of the presence of 'My most dear and loving wife' at his bedside to make his will of which he appointed her the sole executrix. He bequeathed to her the life-interest in one-half of his lands, with the reversion of these to his brother Robert, who was also left the remaining half. Frances was also to receive the rest of his goods and chattels after a complex series of bequests had been met. The beneficiaries included relatives, friends, medical attendants, servants and creditors of himself and his father. To his younger brother Thomas there were to go lands of the value of £100 annually. To his sister, the Countess of Pembroke, he left his best jewel and to the Queen (less deserved) one of £100 value. His uncles Leicester and Warwick were each left £100, and jewels to their Countesses. His books were divided between Dyer and Greville. Walsingham and his wife were each left £100 to buy such things 'as pleaseth them to wear for my remembrance'. And characteristically he begs Sir Francis to take steps for the release of his servant Stephen, a prisoner in Dunkirk, who has 'lain so long in misery'. How his heart would have bled for the victims of concentration camps in the present century!

On the same day he sent for Mr Gifford, a well-known preacher in the camp. With him and other ministers of religion he discussed the question of immortality as expounded both by Greek and Biblical writers. He composed a poem, *La Cuisse Rompue*, relating to his wound, which was set to music and sung to him; and he wrote a long epistle 'in very pure and eloquent Latin' to the learned Belarius, which was afterwards shown to the Queen. The poem and the epistle have been lost, but a last note in Latin on October 16th is known. It is to Johan Wyer, the physician resident at the Court of the Duke of Cleves.

Mi weire veni, veni, de vita periclitor et te cupio. – Nec vivus nee mortuus ero ingratus. Plura non possum sed obnixe oro ut festines. Vale. Arnemi. Tuus. Ph. Sidney.

The note was entrusted to Wyer's nephew, Gisbert Enerwitz, who also wrote urging him to come. But it was too late. Mortification had set in, and even the presence of his brother Robert was too great a strain, and there came what Greville calls 'the last scene of this tragedy . . . the parting between the two brothers, and Philip's final admonition:

Love my memory, cherish my friends; their faith to me may assure you they are honest. But above all govern your will and affections by the Will and Word of your Creator; in me beholding the end of this world with all her vanities.

It is an impressive and saintly farewell, but it is puzzling that Frances is missing from the scene. The end came between two and three p.m. of the next day, October 17th, 1586.

# CHAPTER XXVIII

# NATIONAL GRIEF AND TRIBUTES – THE FUNERAL

It was not till November 2nd that the news reached and shocked England, for no boat had been able to leave Flushing for Sidney's home country for twenty days. Meanwhile the Dutch expressed their deep concern at his loss. The Burgomaster and Council of Flushing sent messages of sympathy to Walsingham, recording their deep indebtedness to Philip and Lady Sidney. The States of Zeeland made a magnanimous but unsuccessful application to Leicester that they might bury him at their own great expense. On October 23rd his body was brought from Arnheim to Flushing where it lay in state in his house for eight days, and was then escorted by the garrison to the waterside with the mourning burghers following. It was embarked in a vessel that had belonged to him, *The Black Pinnace*, whose sails and tackling were throughout black, and which landed at Tower Hill on November 5th. From there his body was carried to the Church of the Minories.

Leicester mingled his grief with that of the Walsinghams when he wrote:

> For mine own part I have lost, beside the comfort of my life, a most principal stay and help in my service here, and, if I may say it, I think none of all hath a greater loss than the Queen's Majesty herself. Your sorrowful daughter and mine is here with me at Utrecht till she may recover some strength, for she is wonderfully overthrown through her long care since the beginning of her husband's hurt, and I am the more careful that she should be in some strength ere she take her journey unto England, for that she is with child.

Here is first-hand testimony to Lady Sidney's assiduous attendance at her husband's sickbed, of which there is no hint in Greville's narrative or even in Philip's last recorded utterances.

The usually unemotional Burghley wrote in similar vein to Walsingham, especially regarding Lady Sidney.

You do very well to provide as much comfort as you can for the young lady, your daughter, considering that, as I hear, she is with child . . . God comfort you and my lady, your wife, as I would have wished it for me and mine.

The loftiest note of all was struck by Lord Buckhurst who had sacrificed his early poetic and dramatic promise to the cares of official life. He wrote to Leicester:

With great grief do I write these lines unto you, being thereby forced to renew to your remembrance the decease of that noble gentleman your nephew, by whose death not only your Lordship and all other his friends and kinsfolk, but even her Majesty and the whole realm besides do suffer no small loss and detriment. Nevertheless it may not bring the least comfort unto you that as he hath both lived and died in fame of honour and reputation to his name in the worthy service of his prince and country, and with as great love in his life, and with as many tears for his death as ever any had, so hath he also by his good and godly end so greatly testified the assurance of God's infinite mercy towards him, as there is no doubt but that he now liveth with immortality, free from the cares and calamities of mortal miseries.

Buckhurst's reference to the Queen's loss was no mere figure of speech. With a belated sense of grief on hearing of Sidney's death she was unable for some days to transact public business. Even the equivalent of 'the ranks of Tuscany' (in Macaulay's phrase) joined in the mourning. The Spanish Ambassador Mendoza, while glad that his sovereign had lost a dangerous enemy, lamented that 'Christendom was deprived of so rare a light in these cloudy times' and bewailed 'poor widow England'. And King Philip inscribed on the despatch, 'He was my godson.'

Then followed the last of the paradoxical episodes which are so singular a feature of Sidney's career. During his resi-

dence in the Netherlands he had added considerably to his
financial indebtedness. But he thought that he had provided
against this by giving Walsingham a power of attorney to
sell part of his lands. But there were legal difficulties and
Walsingham found himself committed to an expenditure of
£6,000, bringing him, he told Leicester, into 'a most hard
and desperate state, which I weigh nothing in respect of the
loss of the gentleman who was my chief worldly comfort . . .
[It] doth greatly afflict me that a gentleman that hath lived
so unspotted a reputation, and had so great care to see all
men satisfied, should be so exposed to the outcry of his
creditors. His goods will not suffice to answer a third part
of his debts already known.'

Walsingham therefore postponed the funeral till after
Leicester's return from the Netherlands and till some further
settlement could be made with the creditors. It took place
on February 16th, 1587, and was on a spectacular scale, as
described by Thomas Lant in his introduction to the Funeral
Roll of Sidney, designed by him and engraved by Derick T.
de Brie. In the procession from the Minories to St Paul's
there were 700 mourners who had difficulty in making their
way through the crowds of sympathetic sightseers in the
streets.

At the head came thirty-two poor groomsmen, each for
one year of Sidney's life. They were followed by officers of
his foot and horse regiments. Then came his standard em-
broidered with the Cross of St George and porcupines and
his device *Vix ea nostra voco*. Sixty of his gentlemen and
yeomen followed, and behind them his chief physician and
surgeon, and his steward. Next came esquires and Knights
among his kinsfolk and friends, including Sir Francis Drake,
and after them the preacher of the funeral sermon, with two
chaplains. Then came the bearer of a pennon with the Sidney
arms, preceding two of his horses, ridden by pages, one
trailing a broken lance, the other carrying a battle-axe reversed. Another standard-bearer went before the Heralds
carrying the insignia of his Knighthood, after whom came
Clarenceux – King-at-Arms.

The coffin with a valvet pall was carried by fourteen of
Sidney's yeomen, and the corners were held by Fulke Gre-

ville, Edward Dyer, Edward Wotton and Thomas Dudley. Behind it as chief mourner walked Robert Sidney, and after him his younger brother Thomas, with other kinsfolk. Gentlemen ushers preceded a group of noblemen on horseback, including Leicester, Pembroke and Essex. After them came representatives of the States of Holland, followed by the Lord Mayor of London in his robes, with the City Sheriff, aldermen and officials, and 120 members of the Company of Grocers, walking in pairs. The procession was closed by about 300 citizens of London trained to bear arms, marching three and three, with weapons reversed.

The Cathedral was hung with black, and after the funeral sermon the body was carried from the choir and buried in the upper north-east end of the choir aisle. A double volley was fired by soldiers in the churchyard.

Sidney's death was the signal for an unprecedented outpouring of elegiac verse and prose, the former in various tongues. The two Universities vied with each other in celebrating his memory. For Cambridge Alexander Neville edited *Academiae Cantabrigiensis Lachrymae*, which appeared with a dedication to Leicester on February 16th, 1587, the day of Sidney's funeral. The contents were almost entirely in the classical tongues, but James VI of Scotland contributed an English sonnet, with a Latin translation. Oxford followed with *Peplus Illustrissimi Viri D. Philippi Sidnaei*, written, somewhat strange to say, by twenty-nine members of New College with which Sidney had no personal connexion, and dedicated to Pembroke. Miss Mona Wilson has pointed out that the title page of this 1587 volume, showing shepherdesses and Amazons crowning a bust of Sidney, and the inscription *Arcadia*, is evidence to the widespread popularity of the old *Arcadia*.[1]

Then in the same year appeared *Exequiae Illustrissimi Equitis D. Philippi Sidnae* with the Oxford University arms on the title page. It had a connexion with Sidney's old College, Christ Church, for it was collected by William Gager. Professor Wallace has called attention to a volume of Latin

[1] *Sir Philip Sidney*, p. 319.

elegies, *Epitaphia in Mortem Nobilissimi et Fortissimi Viri D. Philippi Sidneii,* published at Louvain.[1]

Of the English elegies by individual poets the most note-worthy not for its literary merit, but for its closeness to reality, was that by George Whetstone, dedicated to the Earl of Warwick, with an apology for delay, because he had been anxious to 'publish nothing but truth of so true a Knight'. T. C. Izard has pointed out[2] that to the stanzas in rhyme-royal by 'G. W. Gent' there is added a 'brief Commemoration' in poulter's measure 'of the said right hardy and noble Knight, By B. W. Esquire'. He is George's elder brother, Bernard, who took part in the battle of Zutphen, and Izard suggests that George Whetstone delayed writing his elegy until he could secure first-hand information from his brother. He lays stress on 'hardy Sidney's courage and endurance on the field, charging furiously against the foe'.

> A musket shot his stately horse then slew;
> He, horsed again, the fight did soon renew;
> But Fortune, that at his renown did spight,
> A bullet sent that in his thigh did light.

> \*          \*          \*

> The wound was deep, and shiverèd the bone;
> His heart was good, and manly bare the cross;
> With courage stout he did suppress the moan
> That many made, which did behold his loss.

> \*          \*          \*

> Forth of the field with courage stout he rode.

It is notable too that Whetstone's version of Sidney's last words to his brother Robert is closely akin to that reported by Greville, quoted above:[3]

> Brother (quoth he) to you I must impart
> Three things of weight, impress them in your heart:
> Fear God, and live, love well my friends and know
> That worldly hopes from vanity do flow.

[1] Op. cit., p. 398.
[2] *George Whetstone,* pp. 251–5 (1942).
[3] See p. 187.

We may feel sure from the twofold testimony that we have here authentic witness.

A singular and puzzling contrast is provided by the tribute of a greater poet than Whetstone, Edmund Spenser. *Astrophel. A Pastoral Elegy upon the death of the most Noble and Valorous Knight, Sir Philip Sidney*, dedicated 'to the most beautiful and virtuous Lady, the Countess of Essex'. Both because Spenser had dedicated to Sidney *The Shepheardes Kalender*, and because Sidney was the author of the *Arcadia*, Spenser thought it fitting to cast his elegy into pastoral form. But it was not easy to adjust this to some of the phases of Sir Philip's career and personality. It was possible, of course, to give such a setting to his mental and physical gifts.

> For he could pipe and dance and carol sweet
> Amongst the shepherds in their shearing feast.
>
> \* \* \*
>
> And lays of love he also could compose;
> Thrice happy she, whom he to praise did choose.
>
> \* \* \*
>
> In wrestling nimble, and in running swift,
> In shooting steady, and in swimming strong;
> Well made to strike, to throw, to leap, to lift.
> And all the sports that shepherds are among,
> In every one he vanquished everyone,
> He vanquished all, and vanquished was of none.

But the imagery becomes repellent when the campaign in the Netherlands is transformed into a hunt in a forest waste and wild on foreign soil, where his only care is to kill the savage beasts, and where a cruel one wounds him in the thigh – an incongruously realistic stroke.

Still more disturbing is the transference, if E. de Selincourt's identification is correct, of the name Stella to Sidney's wife, Frances.

> To her he vowed the service of his days,
> On her he spent the riches of his wit,
> For her he made hymns of immortal praise,
> Of only her he sang, he thought, he writ.

Her, and but her, of love he worthy deemed,
For all the rest but little he esteemed.

These lines might have been written of Penelope Devereux, but the Stella in Spenser's poem, like Sidney's wife, hastens to the wounded man's bedside. And when he dies, by a fantastic stretch of poetic licence, her ghost follows his, and together they are transformed into a flower in whose midst a star appeared. As in real life Sidney's widow had become the Countess of Essex, one wonders what she thought of the poem dedicated to her.

# CHAPTER XXIX

# SUMMING-UP

Whatever latitude was allowed by tradition and convention to elegies in verse, a different standard was expected from a memoir in prose. This would particularly apply to an account of Sidney by his lifelong companion and friend, Sir Fulke Greville, Lord Brooke, which he left in manuscript on his death in 1628, and which its latest editor dates between 1610 and 1612.[1] It was published in 1652, with a dedication to the Countess of Sunderland by an unknown P.B., and three-fourths of a century after Sidney's death enshrined him as one of the secular saints of British history. Here is Greville's summing-up of his character at the close of his first chapter.

> The truth is: his end was not writing, even while he wrote; nor his knowledge moulded for tables, or schools; but both his wit and understanding bent upon his heart, to make himself and others, not in words or opinion, but in life and action, good and great. In which architectural art he was such a Master, with so commanding and yet equal ways amongst men, that wheresoever he went he was beloved and obeyed; yea into what action soever he came last at the first, he became first at the last. The whole management of the business not by usurpation or violence but (as it were) by right and acknowledgment falling into his hands, as into a natural centre.

On kindred lines is this tribute in Chapter IV:

> This ingenuity of his nature did spread itself so freely abroad, as who lives that can say he ever did him harm; whereas there be many living that may thankfully acknowledge he did them good. Neither was this in him a private but a public affection; his chief ends being not friends, wife, children, or himself, but above all things the honour of his Maker, and service of his Prince, or country.

In an earlier passage in Chapter III, Greville had expressed

---

[1] Sir Fulke Greville's *Life of Sir Philip Sidney*, edited by Nowell Smith, p. X. (1907)

his hope that Sidney's example would continue to exert its influence after his death.

> Neither am I (for my part) so much in love with this life, nor believe so little in a better to come, as to complain of God for taking him, and such like exorbitant worthiness from us. Yet for the sincere affection I bear to my Prince and country, my prayer to God is, that his Worth and Way may not fatally be buried with him.

Greville may be truly said to have gone far to securing an affirmative answer to his prayer. His treatise, which Nowell Smith justly calls 'at once much less and much more than a biography of Sidney', has given the cue to all later estimates of him as a *Chévalier sans peur et sans réproche*, combining in himself some of the salient features of Medievalism and the Renaissance. And without questioning the fundamental truth of this portraiture, I would suggest that insufficient attention has been given to some of the enigmatic or para-doxical elements in the foregoing chapters.

To begin with, though of course in no way derogatory, it is somewhat disillusioning to learn that the familiar title, Sir Philip, was not bestowed in virtue of his knightly qualities and achievement, but merely as a formality to enable him to act as a proxy for Count Casimir, who was receiving the Garter *in absentia*. It was his good fortune to spend his schooldays at Shrewsbury under Thomas Ashton, one of the most enlightened and stimulating of Tudor headmasters. Yet Sidney's only portrait of a schoolmaster is the blundering, affected Rombus of *The Lady of May*; Ashton was notable for turning the school play into an instrument of education, but not a word is said about this in the discussion of drama in *The Defence of Poesie*. To a young man of Sidney's gifts and temperament the University life of Oxford would pre-sumably make a special appeal, yet he left before taking a degree. Apparently his only allusion by name to a feature of the academic curriculum is when in a letter to his brother Robert he speaks slightingly of 'Ciceroniasm, the chief abuse of Oxford, *Qui dum verba sectantar res ipsas negligunt*. Again there is no mention by him of the plays performed at Oxford when he visited the University in the train of his uncle the

Earl of Leicester, the Chancellor, in 1566 and 1584, though on the latter occasion Gager's tragedy, *Meleager*, must have satisfied his critical standards. *Gorbodne* is the only contemporary play to win from him in *The Defence of Poesie* half-hearted praise. He concedes that *The Mirror for Magistrates* is furnished with beautiful parts, and that *The Shepheardes Calender* has much poetry, in spite of its old rustic language which he cannot approve. The union in the Earl of Surrey of a noble birth and a noble mind helps to procure an encomium on his lyrics, but Sir Thomas Wyatt is passed over in silence.

In Sidney's somewhat acid appraisement of contemporary drama and poetry there is no trace of the impulsiveness which characterized some of his actions in matters of various import. One of the most flagrant instances is his letter to Molyneux, whom he unjustly suspected of betraying to their opponents confidences between himself and his father. 'I assure you before God . . . I will thrust my dagger into you and trust to it, for I speak it in earnest.' Of far weightier moment, and more creditable to his judgment, is his letter to Queen Elizabeth on the projected marriage with the Duke of Anjou, in which he dares to 'set down the over-flowing of my mind in this most important matter, importing, as I think, the continuance of your safety, and, as I know, the joys of my life'.

From a somewhat similar impulse to safeguard a great personage sprang *The Defence of the Earl of Leicester*, a reply to the scurrilous *Leicester's Commonwealth*, an anonymous pamphlet ascribed to the Jesuit Father Parsons. But hurriedly composed it was more a vindication of the Earl's noble lineage than a rebuttal of the crimes laid to his charge, and was not published.

It is tempting to find further evidences of Sidney's impulsiveness in the translations begun and left unfinished by him, the *Psalms*, *The Trewness of The Christian Religion*, Aristotle's *Rhetorie*, perhaps even in the revision of the *Arcadia*. But however this may be, the crowning instance of it was in the rash sympathetic discarding of the piece of armour on his thigh which led to his fatal wound.

Allied to Sidney's impulsiveness was his most serious

defect, his financial improvidence. Throughout his career he was hampered by insufficient means, and was thus often reduced to what now seem to be humiliating petitions for profitable offices. The breadth of Sidney's interests and his aesthetic instincts involved expense and he was dogged by creditors. Before his marriage could take place Walsingham had to undertake to pay his debts up to £1,500, and to promise board and lodging to him and his wife. But more was to follow. After his son-in-law's death Walsingham found that to satisfy what he calls 'his poor creditors' he had to disburse over £6,000, which brought his fortunes very low.

Sidney appointed his 'most dear and loving wife' the sole executrix of his will, and she nursed him zealously during his last illness. There is no evidence that their marriage was unsuccessful. But among Sidney's family letters there is none to her, before or after their wedding. In Greville's account of the last scene of Philip's tragedy it is not Frances, as might have been expected, but his brother Robert who receives his valedictory words. And when she became a widow she twice re-married, the Earl of Essex in 1590, and the Earl of Clanricarde in 1603.

But the more favourable the verdict that can be passed on Sidney's brief married life, the more difficult it is to fit the *Astrophel and Stella* episode into the whole orbit of his career. Were it not for that group of sonnets and songs there would apparently be nothing to connect the names of Philip Sidney and Penelope Devereux after she became Lady Rich. Yet Elizabeth's Court was full of eyes and tongues alert for amorous scandals. As Spenser phrased it in *Colin Clout's Come Home Again*:

> For all the walls and windows there are writ,
> All full of 'love, and love and love my dear',
> And all their talk and study is of it,
> Nor any there doth brave or valiant seem
> Unless that some gay mistress' badge he bears,
> Nor anyone himself doth right esteem
> Unless he swim in love up to the ears.

When Sir Henry Sidney commends Philip as a model to

his brother Robert he does not think of him as the impassioned lover of another man's wife. When Walsingham welcomes him as a suitor for his daughter, he was concerned with the state of his finances, not of his heart. In all this Sir Sidney Lee might have found support for his view that Elizabethan sonnets were literary exercises and had no autobiographical roots. And the complete detachment of *Astrophel and Stella* from the other Sidney material, documentary or literary, remains something of an enigma. But the cumulative internal evidence insists on its basis in fact. And whatever the cost may have been to Philip Sidney, posterity has to be grateful for its rich poetic outcome.

Thus inevitably in the end we surrender to Sidney's fascination. After the *advocatus diaboli* has had his say, this unique Elizabethan's superlative personal magnetism, in itself a form of genius, maintains its triumphant sway. It is doubtful if any other personage in our history can summon such a cloud of witnesses on his behalf. Often a man's severest critics are those of his own household. But his father was always anxious, when possible, to have him at his right hand and for his brothers to take him as their example. It was to Robert that he gave his dying admonition. For his dear lady and sister, the Countess of Pembroke, he wrote and partly re-wrote his *Arcadia*, and it was she who made it her care to superintend the posthumous issues of his works. Between him and his uncle Leicester there was the tie of affection which led Sidney to spring to the defence of his slandered reputation. Most significant of all was his father-in-law's statement, while faced with the heavy burden of his debts, that he weighed them nothing 'in respect of the loss of the gentleman who was my chief worldly comfort'.

Outside the family circle were the intimate personal friends, Fulke Greville, Edward Dyer, Edward Wotton, besides others less closely related who showed their admiration by dedicating books to him, such as Richard Hakluyt and Edmund Spenser. The tributes of English officials, Burghley and Buckhurst, have been quoted. But more remarkable is the devotion he inspired among foreigners, headed by Hubert Languet and Du Plessis Mornay. And William of Orange not only wrote to Elizabeth, highly commending Sidney, but even entertained a project for bestowing his sister's hand upon him.

Elizabeth would never have sanctioned such a union. It is one of the paradoxes of the story of Philip Sidney that his Queen, usually so susceptible to masculine graces, was proof till his loss against his widely tested overpowering attraction. It is the classic example in our history of the proverbial exception that proves the rule.

Cut off before his time towards the close of 1586 Sidney was in one respect fortunate in the date of his death. It was just on the verge of the two greatest achievements of Elizabeth's reign – the defeat of the Armada, and the beginning with Kyd, Marlowe and Shakespeare of its crowning dramatic glories. Thus Sidney stands out as the most representative figure in his complex activities of the earlier decades of Elizabeth's reign. Within the short span of thirty-two years he adorned the age at an astonishing variety of points. He was courtier, statesman, poet, novelist and critic. If fortune had not been perverse, he would have won fame as an explorer and more strictly military laurels than those on the field of Zutphen. It has truly been said that in the variety of his gifts and in his almost mysterious permanent attraction his nearest parallel is no living contemporary but Shakespeare's Hamlet. As this commentary has in part recalled, he has down the centuries evoked admiring interpretation in widespread quarters. It is significant and highly fitting that 1954, the four-hundredth anniversary of his birth, should have been celebrated by an exhibition in the Town Hall of Tunbridge Wells of treasures from Penshurst associated with the name and fame of Philip Sidney. And in the Elysian Fields he will have been glad to know that on November 29th, 1954, the four-hundredth eve of his birthday date, a copy of his portrait was unveiled in Shrewsbury School by Lord De L'Isle and Dudley, his direct descendant through that maternal line, to which he claimed that it was his chiefest honour to belong.[1]

---

[1] Lord De L'Isle and Dudley also opened on November 6th, 1954, an exhibition of books by, or connected with, Sidney and some related objects in the Bodleian Library, Oxford, on which is the article by Mr John Buchan in *The Bodleian Library Record*, July 1955

# INDEX OF PERSONS